Teacher Appraisal
A Practical Guide for Schools

Teacher Appraisal
A Practical Guide
for Schools

Mel West
Cambridge Institute of Education

Rob Bollington
Bedfordshire Education Authority

David Fulton Publishers
London

David Fulton Publishers Ltd
2 Barbon Close, London WC1N 3JX

First published in Great Britain by
David Fulton Publishers 1990

British Library Cataloguing in Publication Data

West, Mel
  Teacher appraisal: a practical guide for schools.
  1. Teachers. Assessment
  I. Title   II. Bollington, Rob
  371.144

  ISBN 1-85346-143-1

Typeset by Chapterhouse, Formby
Printed in Great Britain by BPCC Wheatons Ltd, Exeter

Contents

Introduction vii

Section One   The Purposes Served by Performance Appraisal
              Systems.. 1

Section Two   The Components of Teacher Appraisal.............. 13
              Preparing for the Appraisal Interview............ 17
              The Appraisal Interview............................. 37
              Follow-up Activities................................. 45

Section Three The Management of Teacher Appraisal............. 53

Section Four Support Documentation................................ 63

Section Five Monitoring and Evaluation............................ 69

References 77

Appendix 1   Sample Documents..................................... 79

Appendix 2   Code of Practice....................................... 93

Key Points Index 99

Notes 101

Acknowledgements

This book arises from the authors' involvement in the School Teacher Appraisal Pilot Study and, in particular, the evaluation which was based at the Cambridge Institute of Education of the pilot authorities' development work. The authors are therefore indebted to their colleagues in the evaluation team, to the members of the National Steering Group, to the staffs of those authorities piloting teacher appraisal and, above all, to the many teachers from all levels with whom they met during the evaluation. Though the views expressed in the book are our own, we hope that those with whom we have spoken over the past three years will see a reflection of their own views and experiences in its pages.

Introduction

Since the School Teacher Appraisal Pilot Study was launched in 1987, there has been an increasing number of publications in this area. Many of these deal with single aspects of the appraisal process, such as the interview or classroom observation. Others focus on training or preparation activities. There are even some (see Bollington, Hopkins and West, 1990) which seek to locate appraisal within a wider context of school improvement and teacher development.

In planning this book, the authors hoped to meet a somewhat different need from those outlined above. The intention has been to provide in one short volume an overview of the purposes and processes associated with teacher appraisal, and to express these in terms which give practical advice to those who will be most affected – the appraisers and appraisees in the teaching community. The consideration given to each component part of the process is therefore necessarily abbreviated, though we would hope not partial or simplistic. The emphasis has been placed on the school situation with a series of suggestions about 'getting started', and we would hope that it is possible to dip into this book for ideas which help the actual implementation of appraisal in schools. Though, at the time of writing, we do not as yet know when teacher appraisal will be implemented as a part of the teacher's contract, it is clear that the government's commitment to bring forward appraisal, coupled with enthusiasm for developmental appraisal which emerged from both teacher unions and the LEA employers during the pilot scheme, will make its early introduction both inevitable and desirable. We hope those reading this book will find in it a meaningful contribution to their own thinking and planning processes as implementation draws near.

MEL WEST
ROB BOLLINGTON
Cambridge 1990

SECTION ONE

The Purposes Served by Performance Appraisal Systems

This section examines the development of appraisal schemes. It focuses on the role of appraisal in supporting organisational goals and facilitating staff deployment and development. It then considers the purposes served by teacher appraisal, summarising the views expressed in recent reports; it goes on to suggest a set of objectives for the appraisal scheme which could be adapted to suit the individual school.

The Purposes Served By Performance Appraisal Systems

The development of the role of appraisal schemes

During the evaluation of the School Teacher Appraisal Pilot Study (ESTAPS) it became clear that teachers had mixed feelings about the purposes of appraisal – both what these might be and whether, realistically, they could be achieved. Though all six pilot schemes had adopted the statement of 'nature and purpose' set out in the ACAS agreement (ACAS Appraisal/Training Working Group, 1986) individual teachers were not necessarily aware of its contents. They were, however, aware of the new conditions of service for teachers which provided for the introduction of appraisal within an 'agreed national framework', and many were suspicious about the motives underpinning this provision. It is important therefore to consider the purposes which can be served by staff appraisal, to reassure teachers from the outset, and to establish the real benefits which appraisal can offer to teachers and to schools, and therefore ultimately to pupils. Historically, the major purposes for introducing staff appraisal schemes (Cummings and Schwab, 1973) can be seen as falling into two distinct but related categories:

- Maintaining clear direction and purpose in the organisation
- Evaluating how the organisation's staff resources are being utilised and developing and improving the skills and career prospects of individual staff members.

Maintaining clear direction

In any organisation it is necessary to coordinate the efforts and behaviour of its members towards a series of organisational goals. This does not necessarily imply hierarchy, though most often some form of hierarchical structure is adopted.

3

What this structure seeks to do is to ensure that maximum effort is directed towards the agreed goals of the organisation. At its most straightforward, this may simply be the process of agreeing priorities for individuals and groups, and ensuring that these priorities are communicated (together with the necessary resources) to those expected to secure them.

As organisations grow in size and complexity, however, the process becomes correspondingly complex. Further difficulties can arise from the understanding of the relationships between means and ends – where these are not readily demonstrable the problem of where to devote energies and efforts increases.

As all teachers are aware, the educational system is currently undergoing reforms which are unprecedented both in pace and scope. A central feature of these reforms is the level of prescription: increasingly the goals for schools – curricular, assessment and now financial – are being determined outside the school. Though, inevitably, this causes initial anxiety within school communities, it is a change which may be as beneficial as it is irresistible, since it can be seen as providing school staffs with a clear set of expectations. The *effectiveness* of the school will be related to the extent to which it meets these expectations: that is, whether or not it is able to meet its agreed organisational goals. If it is to do this then, now as never before, it will be necessary to ensure that there are structures and processes within the school which enable the transmission of these priorities to individual teachers and the channelling of individual effort toward these.

Appraisal has a major contribution to make here. First, because appraisal is essentially a dialogue between the different levels of the organisation (about goals, roles, tasks and achievements) it provides opportunity for a structured discussion of how organisational effectiveness can best be pursued, at all levels and by all members of the organisation.

Second, because this dialogue is two-way, it can facilitate the clarification and refinement of organisational goals in the light of real constraints and opportunities.

Third, in providing for these discussions to take place, it will bring an opportunity to review current structures, roles and relationships. In particular there will be the possibility of matching more closely *the authority to act* with the *accountability for organisational goal achievement* which individual teachers carry, and of eliminating the confusion and overlapping of accountabilities whilst ensuring that all necessary decisions have a clear 'home' within the structure.

Evaluating how appropriately staff resources are being used and developed

If the school's *effectiveness* will be determined in the first instance by how appropriate its goals are and how closely these relate to the expectations upon it, its overall performance will also be influenced by its *efficiency* – that is, the way in which it sets about achieving goals, the way resources are deployed. Clearly, the teacher is the most important resource available within the school, therefore the pattern of and support for teacher development will be the most important determinant of the school's efficiency. Appraisal encourages the school – in partnership with the teacher – to look at individual performance, to consider how and where performance can be developed and improved. Further, it provides for feedback in both directions: feedback which is vital to organisational and individual development. The organisation for example, will have a clearer picture of the strengths and interests of the individual teacher; this can lead to better planning, distribution and balancing of roles and tasks. The individual teacher in turn receives feedback from the environment – feedback which has enormous motivational potential, as well as being an important method of reducing the stress and internal tension which individuals often experience at work in the absence of such feedback. It has been argued (Cummings and Schwab, 1973) that feedback to individuals about their performance can influence both the personal constructs which effect performance levels and the individual's perception of the linkages between key variables – ability and performance, for instance, or motivation and performance. Potentially, then, appraisal can help individuals to focus on how best to go about the job – in a way which contributes to organisational goals (*effectiveness*) whilst enabling them to meet individual goals (*personal achievement*). It also permits dialogue about methods and approaches which can lead to a better use of human and other resources (*efficiency*), often as a result of increased self-determination by the individual (*job-satisfaction and motivation*). Appraisal has spread throughout the private sector principally because of the benefits claimed above, though it must be recognised that in a number of organisations a third aspect of the appraisal scheme relates to its role in the determination of individual pay levels. This aspect has not, however, been explored within the trialling of teacher appraisal, and so will not be considered further here, though it remains an issue which excites interest in some quarters, and may well be placed firmly on the agenda of teacher appraisal within the near future.

The purposes of teacher appraisal

When considering the specific purposes of teacher appraisal, there is a large (and rapidly increasing) range of materials available. As more schools and LEAs 'publish' their own views, it becomes increasingly difficult to keep track. However, though there seems to be a rich variety of terms and language used, the central thrust of teacher appraisal, its major points of focus, its component parts and its overriding goals seem reassuringly similar. There are, of course, a number of differences in emphasis between the schemes currently being promoted by different LEAs. There are also a number of national perspectives which would seem to demand particular consideration by those LEAs planning teacher appraisal schemes, which are addressed below.

Teachers' Dispute ACAS Independent Panel: Report of the Appraisal/Training Working Group (ACAS)

The ACAS agreement (1986) listed a set of purposes for teacher appraisal which formed the basis for subsequent trialling of appraisal schemes within the six LEAs whose schemes were funded during the DES 'pilot' project. These were as follows:

● Planning the induction of Entry Grade teachers and assessing their fitness to transfer to the MPG
● Planning the participation of individual teachers in in-service education
● Helping individual teachers, their head teachers and their employers to see when a new or modified assignment would help the professional development of individual teachers and improve their career prospects
● Identifying the potential of teachers for career development, with an eye to their being helped by appropriate in-service training
● Recognition of teachers experiencing performance difficulty, the purpose being to provide help through appropriate guidance, counselling and training. Disciplinary procedures would remain quite separate, but might need to draw upon relevant information from the appraisal records
● Staff appointment procedures. The relevant elements of appraisal should be available to better inform those charged with responsibility for providing references.

The Report of the National Steering Group (NSG) on the School Teacher Appraisal Pilot Study

In the Autumn of 1989 the NSG produced their report on the six teacher appraisal pilot schemes (*School Teacher Appraisal – A National Framework*). In this the aims and purposes for appraisal put forward by the ACAS report were endorsed (with the exception of the recommendation relating to the induction of new teachers, which the NSG felt should be handled separately from any general appraisal scheme).

In particular the NSG singled out the following as appropriate aims for any teacher appraisal scheme:

- Improving the confidence and morale levels of teachers
- Improving communications and professional relations within schools
- Improving the planning and delivery of the curriculum
- Increasing participation in in-service training
- Improving the 'targeting' of in-service training
- Helping teachers with career planning
- Contributing to better informed references.

More generally, the NSG recognised that appraisal should become an 'integral part of the management and support of teachers and must not be treated as an isolated exercise', thus underlining the need for the aims and purposes of any appraisal scheme to be enmeshed into the overall aims and purposes of the school.

Developments in the Appraisal of Teachers – A report by HMI

In October 1989 HMI produced a report based on a 'survey' of appraisal related activities in a range of LEAs, which included those six specifically piloting the teacher appraisal schemes funded by the DES.

The Report notes that in many cases LEAs and schools had not 'fully articulated the purposes of appraisal', and cautions against the launch of a national scheme before securing 'a very large measure of common understanding throughout schools and LEAs about the aims to be pursued through appraisal'.

Nevertheless, HMI identify three major aims for teacher appraisal which emerged consistently at the institutional level:

● *The professional development of teachers*
This was most often expressed in terms of improving the impact of INSET on professional development, with clearer identification of INSET needs and raising the performance of teachers seen as important outcomes. Raising teacher morale and motivation, increasing job satisfaction, clearer identification of the strengths and weaknesses of individual teachers, and providing support were also listed as important teacher-focused goals.

● *Improving the management of the school or college*
HMI reported a growing proportion of institutions perceiving appraisal as providing opportunities for institutional development and change. There was a belief that communication – both in terms of increasing teachers' understanding of the issues confronting senior management and of improving senior managements' understanding of teacher perceptions – would benefit as a result of staff appraisal. Monitoring and review functions could also be carried out more effectively. There was also evidence that appraisal stimulated the production of meaningful job descriptions.

● *Improving classroom performance*
The third group of aims related to improving the quality of teaching and learning. These aims seemed particularly evident within the primary sector, where the specific classroom goals pursued by individuals had often been carefully derived from agreed whole-school policies.

The report also suggests that modifications to the job or role of the teacher have been an important outcome from appraisal, in pilot and non-pilot LEAs alike.

There are then, significant areas of agreement within these reports. The appraisal of teachers is seen as essentially a *developmental process*, not a narrow checking activity, though the quality of development achieved must be influenced by the accuracy of available information concerning past performance, present constraints and opportunities, and future policies. In this context, appraisal itself can be seen as part of the teacher's professional development, not simply a means of identifying development needs.

But there is also an important management link – appraisal (done properly) should lead to improvements in management structures, understanding and performance, as well as enhancing teacher professionalism. The Secretary of State has underlined this double focus in a speech to the Secondary Heads Association (MacGregor, October 1989):

> Appraisal clearly has the potential to strengthen and develop the quality both of teaching and of management in schools in ways which will lead over time to better education for pupils. The National Steering Group point to benefits such as increased confidence for teachers, better curriculum planning, better targeted in-service training and better references for teachers applying for new posts. HMI agree, and state that carried out well, appraisal 'has had a marked effect on the performance of individual teachers'.
>
> I am clear that appraisal is also an important tool for the managers of schools, as it is for management in industrial and commercial firms, and in other occupations. It should provide an opportunity for individual teachers and heads to explore ways of improving their professional skills, and enhancing their contribution to the overall management and development of their school.

But, because each school is different, the particular impact of appraisal is likely to vary accordingly. Even within nationally agreed guidelines one can expect some differences in emphasis, approach and focus according to local considerations. It will be important, therefore, to consider how each school might blend its own goals and priorities into the purposes of appraisal.

Teacher appraisal at LEA, school and teacher levels

An important lesson from the teacher appraisal pilot schemes was that appraisal becomes most beneficial when it ceases to be regarded as a separate activity, but is viewed rather as a vehicle which can help the school and the teacher to plan, prepare for and to implement other major policy initiatives. It is vital, then, from the outset, that appraisal is not conceived as a 'bolt-on' extra. Where it is, it will inevitably fail to secure the purposes underpinning its introduction and, worse, will further squeeze the already over-crowded working hours of teachers. Hostility and resentment can be expected in these circumstances. *Planning* for appraisal therefore needs to be carried forward in the light of the full range of demands confronting the particular LEA, the particular school, the particular teacher. The introduction of the National Curriculum, for example, could be significantly eased if the appraisal process is used to identify what changes will be necessary at school and teacher level and how and by whom these can best be achieved. Similarly, appraisal is capable of providing much of the data necessary for the production of a realistic School Development Plan (SDP), since the important part of the planning will not be identifying appropriate curriculum development goals but identifying who will be able to deliver these, and what preparation and support will be necessary if they are to deliver.

Indeed, it is this facilitative role of appraisal which has prompted dismay in some quarters over the Secretary of State's decision to delay its introduction because 'You cannot do everything at once, the system can only cope with so much' (MacGregor, 1989).

Far from seeing appraisal as an additional burden, John Heywood of the Secondary Heads Association argues that

> A nationally agreed framework for appraisal provides the key to the implementation of the Education Reform Act, and the National Curriculum in particular. ('Taking a Long Look', *Education Guardian*, Oct 1989)

This view was echoed by the appraisal co-ordinator in one of the pilot authority schools:

> If I had been . . . asked which initiative I would have liked to put off it would certainly not have been teacher appraisal. The central aim of appraisal is the improvement of the teacher. The delivery of the National Curriculum, the implementation of local management of schools and assessment of pupils all hang on that. (*Education Guardian*, Oct 1989)

The challenge would seem to be *how*, at LEA, school and teacher levels, appraisal can be introduced without distorting the agenda for major educational reform. It is therefore crucial that a clear set of objectives for teacher appraisal be established, so that those responsible for planning educational change are able to identify how and where the appraisal process will serve the changes. It would be particularly helpful if the objectives could also be expressed in terms which make sense to schools and to teachers, so that at all levels staff know what they should be working towards. The table (Figure 1. 1) is an attempt to produce such a list: not comprehensive, not immutable, but, hopefully, a useful starting point for those embarking upon teacher appraisal within the school.

In order to create a climate in which the objectives in Figure 1. 1 can be realised, it will be necessary to ensure that:

● the appraisal scheme is properly resourced, and schools and teachers are prepared for its introduction;

TEACHER APPRAISAL OBJECTIVES

For the LEA

- [ ] To provide an overall picture of INSET needs and priorities.
- [ ] To help schools to think and to talk about whole-school policies, and the relationships between these policies and individual roles and tasks.
- [ ] To facilitate development planning processes and activities in schools.
- [ ] To provide an informed basis for teacher references, and to improve the quality of promotion/selection decisions within the authority.

For the School

- [ ] To ensure that individual targets/objectives relate to school objectives and priorities.
- [ ] To help individuals improve performance in their current jobs.
- [ ] To improve communication and relationships.
- [ ] To increase teacher involvement in determining, and commitment to securing, their own targets.
- [ ] To identify individual strengths and weaknesses and improve the match between individual skills and organisational tasks.
- [ ] To improve the quality of information on which INSET planning is currently based.
- [ ] To identify interest in and potential for promotion to specific jobs, and to help individuals to prepare for this.

For the Teacher

- [ ] To increase the scope for personal achievement, job satisfaction and, where appropriate, career development.
- [ ] To improve working relationships with colleagues.
- [ ] To provide balanced, objective feedback on previous performance, and guidance, support, reassurance and motivation for the future.
- [ ] To provide opportunity to express views about the school, or how it is managed, in the expectations that appropriate action will be taken where possible and necessary.

Figure 1.1

- information arising from the appraisal process (at all levels) is seen to influence subsequent decision-making and patterns of resource use;
- the confidentiality of appraisal dialogues and documentation is guaranteed.

SECTION TWO

The Components of Teacher Appraisal

This section explores the major components of the appraisal process. It begins with an overview of these processes, and then considers in some detail what is involved in preparing for, carrying out and following up on appraisal activities. Its purpose is to flag the main issues for appraisers and appraisees, and to suggest ways in which these might be tackled.

The Components of Teacher Appraisal

An analysis of appraisal schemes (in both public and private sector settings) suggests that typically three broad stages are involved:

(1) Preparation
(2) Interview
(3) Follow-up

The interview is typically the central point and provides an opportunity for appraiser and appraisee to discuss the appraisee's work and how it fits into the school's policies and priorities. Good interview practice is usually held to involve a review of work done since the previous appraisal and planning or target-setting for the future. Increasingly, interviews have been seen as simply one event in a continuous and developing relationship. They have also increasingly been portrayed as a two-way process, where the emphasis is on *joint* problem-solving and development in the context of authentic dialogue.

The success of appraisal interviews has been seen, for the most part, to hinge on effective preparation. Therefore, steps need to be taken to ensure that the discussions during the interview are based on information about the appraisee's work which has been systematically gathered and organised and properly considered.

However, if all that appraisal consists of is an exchange of information and a discussion of its significance, then something important will be lost. The aim should be for the interview to result in agreed action plans and targets for the future. Further, both parties should emerge from the interview with a clear view of what action has been agreed, and their respective responsibilities in relation to this action.

In schools, experience from the early development work has shown that this basic, generic appraisal model of preparation/interview/follow-up can work well. Where there have been difficulties, these can often be traced to a lack of appropriate preparation by one or both parties. A particularly important area for preparation is classroom observation.

Because of the tradition of classroom autonomy, unlike some occupations, the teacher's appraiser will not necessarily have a close and direct view of the teacher's main work. Classroom observation has, therefore, been seen as the major vehicle for producing a more informed view of the teacher's work. It is important to remember, however, that despite its central importance, classroom work is not the whole of a teacher's job, particularly for senior staff. Therefore, in the interest of achieving a balanced and rounded view, other methods of data gathering need to be added to classroom observation. These should be identified and agreed at the beginning of the appraisal process.

The three basic stages in teacher appraisal referred to above are reflected in the model of appraisal recommended by the National Steering Group following the School Teacher Appraisal Pilot Study. In these proposals, the suggested components of the preparation/interview/follow-up model are expanded as in Figure 2.1.

PREPARATION	Initial meeting
	Self-appraisal
	Classroom/task observation
	Collection of other relevant 'data'
INTERVIEW	Interview
	Target-setting
	Production of statement
FOLLOW-UP	Discussions/meetings
	Professional development activities
	Review meeting/additions to statement
	Follow-up support/professional development

Figure 2.1

What is also clear from the pilot study, however, is that while appraisal can be very useful as an aid to planning for the future, the process *in itself* presents valuable developmental opportunities and experiences to those involved. The various preparatory activities, for example, can in themselves lead to improvements in understanding, knowledge and teacher skills, as well as contributing to an effective appraisal process.

The following parts of Section Two will look in more detail at each of these three main stages, and seek to establish practical advice to teachers on how to go about these activities so that the individual teacher and the school can gain maximum benefit.

Preparing for the Appraisal Interview

Overview

In this part of Section Two, we are concerned with activities at the preparation stage of the appraisal process. We believe the quality of effort at this stage can significantly affect the rest of the process. We also believe it can itself provide valuable opportunities for professional development. Careful attention at the preparation stage will help to ensure that the interview is based on informed views as opposed to impressions or hearsay. Appropriate preparatory work may also influence the teacher's attitude towards the rest of the process.

The following discussion is organised around a series of questions which are central to the preparation phase of the appraisal process and which need to be addressed to ensure fairness to, and the goodwill of, the teacher. These questions are:

- What aspects of the teacher's work are to be appraised?
- What information needs to be collected about these aspects of the work in order to promote an informed discussion at the interview, and how can this information best be collected?
- What counts as 'success' in those aspects of the job covered within the appraisal?

What aspects of the teacher's work are to be appraised?

General or selective focus?

A basic decision concerns whether to appraise all, most, or selected aspects of the appraisee's job. The answer here is likely to relate to a number of factors: eg the complexity of the job, time spent in the job, previous appraisals, school and individual priorities. 'Whole job' appraisal seems to prove most beneficial where the teacher is relatively new in the particular post, and where the job is less complex. It can also be a useful approach to the first cycle of the appraisal process. However, for experienced heads and teachers, and those who have previously been appraised, selecting particular aspects of the job for appraisal is likely to prove a more productive use of time and energy.

Factors affecting what is selected for appraisal.

Factors which are likely to affect what is selected for appraisal are shown diagrammatically in Figure 2.2:

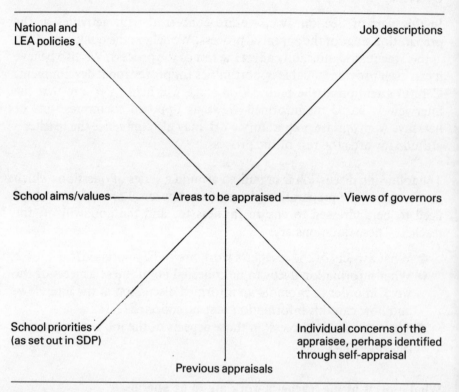

Figure 2.2

Selecting areas for appraisal

STEP 1 Appraisers meet
Following design work on the systems and training at the start of a new appraisal cycle, the head of a large school will need to organise a meeting between the team of appraisers. This meeting will be useful for:

- clarifying the parameters and timescale of the process;
- identifying matters of school concern or priority to be addressed in appraisal;
- establishing a common understanding of the process;
- establishing clarity over procedures, including those of the follow-up-stage.
  (Where the head is the sole appraiser, he or she will need to consider these points and then move on to step 2.)

STEP 2 Staff briefing
The head can then hold a staff meeting to brief all teachers about the process and allow an opportunity for discussion of concerns. This meeting can be used to clarify details of the process and general procedures to be used.

STEP 3 Initial appraiser/appraisee meetings
These meetings are valuable and necessary ways of starting or restarting the appraisal cycle. They provide an opportunity to:
- clarify the process
- explore expectations of and feelings towards appraisal.
- agree aspects of work to be focused on;
- discuss approaches to information gathering;
- agree a timetable and arrangements for the process.

What information needs to be gathered and how can this information best be collected?

Our central point is that a successful appraisal inteview is dependent on building the discussion on a solid basis of relevant factual information. Therefore, data gathering needs to be systematic and purposeful. Information needs to be collected in a balanced and respresentative way to illustrate what is being appraised. To increase the trustworthiness of this information the following steps can be taken:

- use a range of sources of information;
- use a variety of data gathering techniques;
- collect data over an appropriate period of time.

Checklists (a) and (b) in Figure 2.3 serve as guides to the range of possibilities, although we would point out that some of those listed fall outside current appraisal practice in schools, and the use of any particular method of data gathering needs to be agreed with the appraisee.

Checklist (a) Sources of information

PEOPLE	The appraisee	DOCUMENTS	Schemes of work
	Colleagues		Policy statements
	Students/pupils		School brochures
	Parents		
	Governors	ARTEFACTS	Examples of pupils' work
	LEA officials		Classroom display

Checklist (b) Data gathering methods

- ☐ Self-appraisal
- ☐ Task observation/job shadowing
- ☐ Collecting the views of relevant people by interviews/questionnaires
- ☐ Classroom observation
- ☐ Analysing documentation, eg schemes of work, policy statements
- ☐ Looking at pupils' work
- ☐ Analysing test/exam results

Figure 2.3

The lists are intended to serve as the basis of discussion. They are not seen as exhaustive or prescriptive.

The key point is that once the appraiser and appraisee have agreed areas to focus on within the appraisal, they need to survey the range of possibilities available for information gathering and to select those appropriate to their purposes.

A brief discussion of some of the more common approaches to information gathering follows. These are self-appraisal, classroom observation, task observation and collecting colleagues' views.

Self-appraisal

Self-appraisal can be conducted in a variety of ways. Indeed it would be an unusual teacher who did not reflect on his or her work, whether or not there is a formal appraisal scheme. One purpose of appraisal is to encourage this type of reflection and to make it more purposeful and systematic. Beyond this, self-appraisal is a means by which an appraisee can prepare for the various discussions in the formal appraisal process. A variety of approaches can be used; within the School Teacher Appraisal Pilot Study, for example, these varied from 'free writing' to working through detailed prompt lists to thought/reflection which was not recorded in any way.

Purpose: Self-appraisal tends, by prompting deeper thinking about what we do, to increase understanding of the links between behaviour and outcomes. It can also be a useful way of clarifying those areas an individual wishes to address, and in this way stimulate change and development.

Timing: Self-appraisal can be useful at various points in the appraisal process. It can, for example, be used to prepare for the initial meeting in order to help an individual decide which aspects of his or her work to suggest for appraisal. It can also be used for an appraisee to clarify his or her thoughts in readiness for the appraisal interview.

Levels: Self-appraisal can operate on a number of levels. At one level it is no more than setting aside a few quiet moments to think about your work. Alternatively self-appraisal can be carried out in a highly structured and focused manner. For some, continuous self-appraisal is a major vehicle of professional development rather than an isolated event. Indeed, we have found many teachers are highly self-critical and inclined to analyse their own practice in precisely the way a formal appraisal system can support. Clearly the notion of 'reflective practitioners' who analyse their own practice in a balanced way and discuss and exchange ideas freely with colleagues is not new to teachers. It is, however, the matching of what people feel about their own practice with how colleagues see it that contributes to a balanced view and a solid basis for developments and this is what appraisal can facilitate. Appraisers are able to use alternative sources of information to reassure an overly self-critical appraisee, or to point to an individual blindspot, and in this way can extend personal understanding. At the same time, by sharing their reflections, teachers can contribute to increasing the understanding of appraisers.

Approaches: There are a number of possible alternative approaches to structured self-appraisal. These need to be considered from two angles. First, in designing a self-appraisal prompt sheet, there is the question of what aspects of a teacher's job it should cover. Second, there is the technical issue of how the aspects raised in the prompt sheet are turned into questions, and these questions are put together into a self-appraisal form.

1. Aspects for self-appraisal

The first area to discuss is the matter of deciding what a self-appraisal sheet should cover, in terms of drawing attention to **areas or aspects of a** teacher's job. The 1986 ACAS Report of the Appraisal/Training Working Group usefully mapped out the territory by giving some headings, and provides one aid to self-appraisal (see Figure 2.4)

SELF APPRAISAL PROMPT SHEET

(a) The Teacher in the Classroom
      (i) preparation
      (ii) teaching skills
      (iii) follow-up

(b) The Teacher in the School and Community
      (i) pastoral care
      (ii) co-operation and team-work
      (iii) curriculum involvement

(c) The Teacher as Manager
      (i) management skills
      (ii) leadership
      (iii) self-determined professional development

(d) The Teacher in the Future
      (i) further training needed
      (ii) further experience needed
      (iii) potential for additional responsibility
      (iv) career aspirations

Figure 2.4 (Source: ACAS Report Annex D, 1986)

The list suggests *areas* for self-appraisal. The question of the derivation of criteria will be discussed in more detail later. One point to register here is that in designing a self-appraisal form, schools may find it useful to suggest criteria for teachers to consider when evaluating their own performance in particular areas of their work.

2. Designing a self-appraisal form

We now take some of the ideas contained in the ACAS report to illustrate how the design process might be carried out through a number of steps.

STEP 1
Decide on each aspect of the job to be covered in a self-appraisal form
    Example: Teaching skills

STEP 2
Identify criteria which could be used to evaluate this aspect of the job

Example: Teaching skills relate to presentation of material, involvement of pupils, awareness of individual needs, mastery of subject matter, mastery of a variety of teaching techniques, having appropriate standards and expectations, etc.

STEP 3
Decide on ways of indicating success for each criterion
Example: Presentation of materials. 'Measures' are needed in order to determine whether or not materials are being presented well. These could include

- the teacher's ability to give clear, unambiguous and helpful explanations, demonstrations, practice and feedback;
- the teacher's ability to check pupils' comprehension of what is presented;
- the teacher's ability to gear presentations to the pupils' ability, previous experience, comprehension and attention span.

STEP 4
Turn this into a self-appraisal form
These are various alternative designs for self-appraisal forms:

● The 'forced choice' approach
In this model, appraisees are required to select from alternatives the most appropriate answer to a particular question.
Example:

When you present a new topic to a class do the pupils
a) always see links with previous work and experience?
b) see links on some occasions but not others?
c) see some links with previous work and experience, but not the links that are most helpful for them to make?
d) usually find it hard to relate the topic to previous work and experience?
Please select the most appropriate answer and consider the implications.

● The use of open ended questions
Example: What happens when you present a new topic to a class?
● The use of rating scales
Example: When you present a new topic to a class, do the pupils see links with previous work? ... Always/Frequently/Sometimes/Not very often/Never (Please tick as appropriate).

● The use of 'prompts'
   Examples: *Either* My pupils would understand the new topics presented to them better if... *Or* My pupils understand the new topics presented to them best when...
● Self-comparison
   Example:

The following are teaching skills connected with presenting new topics to pupils. Please rank them in order according to which you feel you do best:

☐ Ability to explain new work clearly.
☐ Attention to checking pupils' understanding of new work.
☐ Providing pupils with opportunities to master new work.
☐ Providing pupils with feedback on their progress with new work.
☐ Ability to relate new work to pupils' previous work and experience.

● A blank sheet of paper
   Sometimes just writing down in an unstructured way what you feel about your job can be helpful. Sometimes this task can be facilitated by the suggestion of key points to consider (as in the ACAS example).

These methods can, of course, be used in combinations. For example, teachers may find it helpful to combine self-comparison with rating scales. Whatever the approach, however, the format must be readily undestood and acceptable. Above all, a self-appraisal form is meant to prompt reflection, not place a barrier in the way of it.

Classroom observation

Purposes: A major focus for appraisal is the performance of teachers in the classroom. Informed discussion of a teacher's work here can be considerably enhanced by appropriate classroom observation. However, the relative importance of classroom observation as a form of information gathering is likely to vary according to the teacher's particular job, length of experience and the focus of a particular appraisal cycle. Observation is not straightforward. There are alternative approaches to select from and observation skills need to be developed. It is, however, a potentially rewarding and reassuring activity, with strong motivational possibilities.

Levels: Observation can be general or specific in focus. It can be diagnostic in purpose or emphasise monitoring or evaluation issues. Alternatively it can form the basis of a 'coaching' approach to development. It can be carried out by the teacher him/herself in the form of action research, be done by a peer or by a superior. It is important that there is a clear understanding of how classroom observation will be conducted before it is carried out.

Timing: We see classroom (and indeed task observation), as coming into the appraisal process in two places. Both can be used to gather information in preparation for the interview, or to provide support or monitoring at the follow-up stage. In the latter case, where the interview has resulted in targets linked to classroom work, these might be facilitated by feedback from an observer or monitored by an observer at an agreed point in time.

Methods

(a) Procedure
It is helpful to set observation in between a planning meeting and a feedback session (see Figure 2.5). At the planning meeting the *scope*, the *focus*, the *methods*, and the *context* for the observation are discussed. The initial meeting referred to above may also serve as the planning meeting for the first observation session. The observation can then take place with both appraiser and the appraisee knowing what to expect.

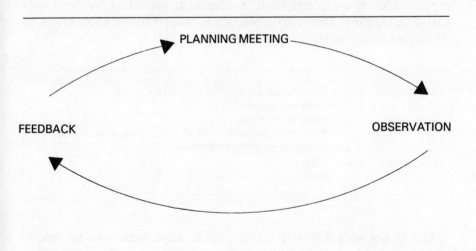

Figure 2.5

The feedback session needs to be approached carefully. Initial feedback needs to be factual and on the agreed areas of observation. The observer needs to avoid rushing in with judgemental comments and must allow time for the appraisee to express his/her views. Above all, feedback needs to be given soon after the lesson – certainly within 48 hours – so that uncertainty and anxiety are avoided. Criteria used to assess or evaluate need to be accepted by both teacher and observer and discussed between them.

(b) Observation methods
(i) Writing notes
The observer can simply note down what happens in the lesson. This approach can be made more manageable and purposeful by noting down what happens under a number of agreed headings. It can be further developed by keeping a record of the times at which various events take place. In this approach, some form of shorthand needs to be used. The aim is to enable the lesson to be reconstructed accurately during later discussion.

(ii) Structured observation
Other approaches to observation make use of some kind of pro-forma on which the observer uses ticks or some other type of abbreviation to record events in the lesson.

The observer might be asked to put down a *tally* every time a particular event occurs. Alternatively, the observer might scan the classroom at regular intevals and *code* what is observed, according to previously agreed categories. The chart summarises these various alternatives to classroom observation.

WRITING NOTES	'Blank sheet of paper' to be used for either • lesson transcript, or • critical incidents. 'Key headings' to allow observer to restrict observation to particular aspects of the lesson.
STRUCTURED RECORDING	Tally Code

This is not an exhaustive list and other approaches can be readily developed within the school, but let us take one aspect of teaching as an example and illustrate it with reference to these approaches in order to show a variety of possibilities. The aspect illustrated here is the way in which a teacher uses *questions* to involve pupils.

Example:

WRITING NOTES
The observer focuses on teacher questioning and pupil response and might note down either examples of approaches used *or* do a transcript of key exchanges in the lesson, which illustrate typical teacher-pupil interactions.

TALLY SYSTEM
The observer designs an observation schedule and puts a tally down every time a particular event occurs. This results in a record of the pattern of classroom activities.

Teacher Questioning	
Questions to class as a whole	IIII
Questions to named individuals	II
Responses from named individuals	I
Responses volunteered by individuals	II

CODING SYSTEM
The observer scans the class at agreed intervals and jots down what is happening according to agreed categories. Again a pattern of classroom activities will be revealed. Figure 2.6 illustrates this approach

(iii) Audio and audio-visual approaches
The use of video or tape recording to aid classroom observation has strengths and weaknesses. Both can be a very powerful means of reconstructing a lesson and enable the teacher to receive very compelling feedback. While these aids are more or less selective in focus, depending on where the machinery is located, they provide accurate, factual data. They can also be used to give a teacher access to feedback without requiring the presence of an observer.

On the other hand, the use of video recorders and tape recorders can seem threatening and distracting and needs to be done sensitively and only where appropriate. Though they record factual information this information will still need to be interpreted later and it is important to explore perspectives on and understanding of the data with the teacher.

Focus = *Teacher–pupil interaction*
Please scan the classroom every 15 seconds and record what you observe, using the following codes:
(a) teacher question to whole class
(b) teacher question to named individuals
(c) response/comment from pupil that is invited
(d) uninvited response/comment of a positive nature
(e) negative/disruptive pupil comment
(f) other

0.15	a	2.45		5.15		etc	
0.30	a	3.00		5.30			
0.45	d	3.15		5.45			
1.00	b	3.30		6.00			
1.15	d	3.45		etc.			
1.30	etc.	4.00					
1.45		4.15					
2.00		4.30					
2.15		4.45					
2.30		5.00					

Figure 2.6

Whatever the approach to classroom observation, in all approaches it is necessary to determine *before the lesson* how the observer will behave, in terms of participating in the lesson or not. Clearly, some approaches make it easier to remain 'a fly on the wall' than others. Our advice is that both participant and non-participant observation can be useful but that in the end the observer's responsibility is to give appropriate feedback. Too much participation can prevent, or at least compromise, this.

In classroom observation, therefore, there are a variety of possible approaches from which to select according to the focus and purpose of the observation. The technique used is not an end in itself but must be judged in terms of how far it promotes a productive feedback discussion, which allows the teacher to learn and progress. It may be that observers will need to use more than one technique in any particular observation.

Feedback

The following advice, given in one of the six pilot LEAs, to observers may be helpful to bear in mind during feedback sessions:

A good observer should:

- allow the teacher to talk;
- check progress towards previously established targets;
- focus on a limited number of areas (not more than three) for remedy/improvement/setting targets;
- ensure careful recording so that commitments and suggestions to support improvements are not lost;
- enable the teacher to diagnose his/her own performance and to suggest future needs and targets;
- leave the teacher wanting to repeat the process.

(Suffolk LEA, 1988)

Observation should lead to a productive discussion and exchange of ideas about those aspects of teaching identified as points of focus during initial planning. This discussion should occur in the feedback session held soon after the observation, though it may raise issues which will receive further attention during the appraisal interview itself. In some models of appraisal, some of the observation may be carried out by peers. If this approach is used the teacher and the observer will need to report to the appraiser on what was learned from the observation, in order to aid the appraiser's preparation for the interview. Sometimes, however, and particularly where the observer is the appraiser, those involved may feel that they have covered the outcomes from classroom observation at the feedback session. They may even feel there is little left to discuss at the appraisal interview. In part this problem can be solved by the availability of other data to inform the interview, in part by seeing the observation data as a source of examples to illustrate or test out more general points to be discussed in the interview. The interview might also be concerned with general findings from a series of observations as opposed to feedback sessions concerned with particular lessons. The interview might alternatively incorporate the final feedback session.

The main aim of the observer should be to collect factual data to present to the teacher. In the first instance, it should be for the teacher to reflect on and interpret the data. Only then should the observer offer interpretations, and these should be on the basis of agreed and known criteria. The aim should be to use the data gathered to lead to plans for future development. Such plans may emerge at the feedback meetings, following the observation, but should be confirmed and possibly refined at the interview itself.

Task observation

Purposes: 'Task' observation can be used to collect data on the carrying out of a teacher's management or pastoral responsibilities. We believe the feedback provided as a result of task observation can be helpful. As with classroom observation, task observation works best if it is planned and purposeful.

Levels: Most of what has been written about classroom observation can be applied here. It is important, again, to be clear on what is to be observed and to select an appropriate method. Success in task observation depends, we believe, on a tight definition of the scope of the process. Vague job shadowing tends to be less productive than a more intensive and focused period of task observation.

Timing: As with classroom observation, task observation can be used to gather data for discussion at the interview or to support and monitor agreed targets or action plans.

Methods

For task observation, it is desirable to ensure:

- the use of a preparation/observation/feedback procedure
- a clear definition of the purposes of the observation
- the use of an appropriate observation schedule.

Task observation schedules can be designed along the same lines as classroom observation schedules. The alternatives, therefore, include making notes, tally, coding, and audio-visual systems.

For example, if a teacher is concerned with his or her performance in running a meeting, the observer might devise a schedule to record what happens in the meeting. Figures 2. 7 and 2. 8 give some idea of how the design of a suitable instrument can be approached. The example is given to suggest the use of a structured approach to task observation and to encourage some flexibility in recording methods. The key aim, as with classroom observation, is for the approach used to enable effective feedback and development.

MEETINGS OBSERVATION SCHEDULE 1

PROPOSING	A behaviour which puts forward a new concept, suggestion or course of action.
BUILDING	A behaviour which extends or develops a proposal which has been made by another person.
SUPPORTING	A behaviour which involves a conscious and direct declaration of support or agreement with another person or his concepts.
DISAGREEING	A behaviour which involves a conscious and direct declaration of difference of opinion, or criticism of another person's concepts.
DEFENDING/ATTACKING	A behaviour which attacks another person or defensively strengthens an individual's own position. Defending/attacking behaviours usually involve overt value judgements and often contain emotional overtones.
BLOCKING/DIFFICULTY STATING	A behaviour which places a difficulty or block in the path of a proposal or concept without offering any alternative proposal and without offering a reasoned statement of disagreement. Blocking/difficulty stating behaviours therefore tend to be rather bald; eg 'It won't work' or 'We couldn't possibly accept that'.
OPEN	A behaviour which exposes the individual who makes it to risk of ridicule or loss of status. This behaviour may be considered as the opposite of defending/attacking, including within this category admissions of mistakes or inadequacies provided that these are made in a non-defensive manner.
TESTING UNDERSTANDING	A behaviour which seeks to establish whether or not an earlier contribution has been understood.
SUMMARISING	A behaviour which summarises, or otherwise restates in a compact form, the content of previous discussion or considerations.
SEEKING INFORMATION	A behaviour which seeks facts, opinions or clarification from another individual or individuals.
GIVING INFORMATION	A behaviour which offers facts, opinion or clarification to other individuals.

Figure 2.7   Outline definitions of behaviour categories (Based on Rackham *et al.*, 1973 and reproduced with permission from Wellens Publishing Co Ltd)

MEETINGS OBSERVATION SCHEDULE 2

PERSONS PRESENT AT MEETING

															TOTAL
PROPOSING															
BUILDING															
SUPPORTING															
DISAGREEING															
DEFENDING/ ATTACKING															
BLOCKING/ DIFFICULTY STATING															
OPEN															
TESTING UNDERSTANDING															
SUMMARISING															
SEEKING INFORMATION															
GIVING INFORMATION															

Figure 2.8 Behaviour analysis observation form (Based on Rackham *et al.*, 1973, and reproduced with permission from Wellens Publishing Co Ltd)

Collecting colleagues' views

Potentially, collecting colleagues' views can provide an appraisee with valuable feedback on how his/her efforts are perceived by others. Except in the case of headteacher appraisal, however, collecting data from colleagues about the appraisee's work was not very common in the School Teacher Appraisal Pilot Study. Partly this reflected the emphasis placed on other forms of preparation but partly it reflected the sensitivity teachers feel about the collection of 'other informed opinion'. Nevertheless, collecting colleagues' views can produce information not otherwise available.

Where it is thought appropriate to seek this kind of data, then care is needed to ensure this is done in a systematic, acceptable and fair manner. Whatever the mechanisms used for collecting views, *how* the process is set up is most important. A code of practice, such as the one included in the National Steering Group's report (NSG, 1989), is highly desirable, and can be a source of guidance to appraisers (see Appendix 2). There also needs to be a clearly understood set of processes.

We would suggest the following stages are followed in collecting colleagues' views on a teacher's work:

(1) Appraiser and appraisee agree aspects of job to be appraised.
(2) Appraiser and appraisee agree what information is needed to hold an informed discussion about these aspects.
(3) Appraiser and appraisee agree appropriate ways of collecting the necessary information.
(4) If colleagues are to be approached for information, appraiser and appraisee agree:

   - who is to be approached? when?
   - what is each person to be asked?
   - how are they to be asked? (questionnaire, interview, etc)
   - what records/notes will be made?
   - what rules of confidentiality will be applied?
   - what steps are needed to brief those to be approached?

(5) Appraiser and appraisee need to agree a time for feeding back and discussing the information gathered. This could either be at the appraisal interview, or at an agenda-setting meeting which takes place before the interview.

What counts as success in each aspect of the job chosen for appraisal?

At some stage in the appraisal process, the information gathered about a person's work will need to be interpreted. Facts will need to be evaluated. This raises the question of what criteria should be used. Schools will need to address this issue and may be helped by advice from a number of sources. Basically, it is possible for them to look to the following sources for advice on criteria:

- Lessons from *research* into effective teaching
- Guidance given in *official* publications (DES, HMI, NCC, LEA, GCSE boards etc.).
- Lessons from the *psychology* of learning and motivation.
- Views of teachers, parents, governors and pupils.
- Previously agreed school policy, school aims and values, School Development Plan priorities.

We would argue that criteria generated in each of these ways are likely to be fairly general. They will need to be adapted to suit a particular setting. As a starting point, we recommend the list of criteria (Figure 2. 9), from the Report of the Appraisal Training Working Group, for appraising teachers. We suggest that this list may serve as the basis of a discussion of

---

PROMPT LIST

It must be stressed that this list is neither prescriptive nor exhaustive and may need modification in the light of experience gained during the Pilot Study.

A.   The Teacher in the Classroom

PREPARATION

The activity was part of a properly planned programme.
The aim of the activity was clear.
A suitable approach was chosen from the options available.
Adequate and suitable resources were available.
The learning environment had been considered.

TEACHING SKILLS

The material was well presented.
The pupils were actively involved.
The teacher
– adapted the approach when necessary;
– was aware of individual needs within the group;
– displayed mastery of the subject matter.

FOLLOW-UP

Homework is regularly set (if appropriate).
Pupils' work is marked and recorded regularly.
Pupils receive appropriate feedback about their work.
Parents are informed of pupils' work and progress in accordance with school policy.
The teacher evaluates the success of his/her teaching.

B. The Teacher in the School and the Community

CARE FOR
INDIVIDUAL
PUPIL

The teacher
– is involved in the pastoral curriculum;
– actively furthers the discipline and aims of the school;
– seeks, in appropriate cases, to liaise with outside agencies, ie EWO, psychologist, etc;
– is involved in structured liaison with parents;
– takes part in extra-curricular activities relevant to the professional development of the teacher.

CO-OPERATION,
TEAMWORK AND
CURRICULUM

The teacher has contributed during the last year to, for example, some or all of the following: syllabus preparation/evaluation, working parties; support for probationers; resource preparation; in-service training; liaison with feeder/receiving schools.
The teacher
– has been involved in team teaching and/or cross-curricular developments;
– has an awareness of the wider curriculum.
The teacher meets deadlines.

C. The Teacher as Manager

MANAGEMENT SKILLS

Where applicable, how does the teacher manage: own time; finance; ancillaries; other teaching staff?

LEADERSHIP

How well does the teacher communicate with colleagues on professional matters; motivate other staff; delegate work to assistant staff; support and advise colleagues; organise the work of a group?

SELF DETERMINED
PROFESSIONAL
DEVELOPMENT

What courses (Teachers' Centre and others) has the teacher attended in the past year? What contribution has been made in any other way to teacher groups?

D. The Teacher in the Future

FURTHER TRAINING
NEEDED

eg classroom management; subject knowledge; general management; pastoral.

FURTHER EXPERIENCE
NEEDED

eg visit other schools; secondment; courses; exchange posts.

POTENTIAL FOR
ADDITIONAL
RESPONSIBILITY

eg administration; committees; curriculum reviews; staff development.

Figure 2.9 (Source: Report of the ACAS Appraisal/Training Working Group, 1986)

what criteria to use within a particular school. We would stress the importance of holding such a discussion as a means of ensuring a common understanding and acceptance of the critera to be applied. It should also ensure that criteria derived from whatever source are modified to fit particular teachers and circumstances.

Summary

The preparation activities we have described can provide many opportunities for professional development. They are, however, primarily intended to ensure that an informed discussion takes place at the appraisal interview.

In practice, both appraiser and appraisee need to prepare for and think about the interview in advance. Lack of preparation by either party can lead to problems at the interview. In order to channel the preparation into an interview discussion, a pre-interview meeting is helpful. This should take place a few days before the interview and enable the appraiser and appraisee to review and agree the interview agenda. It can also be helpful if, between this pre-interview meeting and the interview itself, both appraiser and appraisee note down key points and issues for discussion under each agenda heading. Sometimes this is done by means of an interview preparation form. The major requirement is for both appraiser and appraisee to gather information systematically and then to bring this to bear during the discussion.

The Appraisal Interview

Striking a balance

The appraisal interview is at the heart of the appraisal process. Though there are a wide variety of models of appraisal, featuring different approaches, activities and components, the interview stands out as the one consistent feature of all models.

> Its object has been to review the appraisee's work, identifying successes and areas which could be developed; to identify any training or development needs; and to agree targets for action......We recommend that the Regulations specify clearly that appraisal programmes should in all cases include an interview with the purposes set out above, the substance of which should be recorded in the appraisal statement. (NSG Report, 1989)

The centrality of the interview is hardly surprising, as it is the occasion when the appraisal dialogue takes place, when the information which has been gathered about past performance is considered, and plans are made for the future. However, as is clear from the previous sections, the interview, though central, is by no means the only important activity. Indeed, without appropriate preparation and follow-up activity, it cannot be a meaningful exchange. Nevertheless it occupies a particularly sensitive place in the chain of appraisal processes, and the emphasis which is given within the interview to reviewing the past and to anticipating the future is crucial if appraisal is to be a helpful and developmental experience for those involved. It is worthwhile, therefore, to consider briefly what it is the appraisal interview brings together.

One way of thinking about this is to consider what appraisal is really trying to do; this could be described as looking at the recent past in order to improve decision-making and effectiveness in the foreseeable future. Thus appraisal will always bring with it two components – a review or assessment of what has happened and how the individual has coped in the previous time period, and a plan (or series of plans) for the future, which are informed by and reflect the lessons of the review, as well as meeting known future requirements. It is unwise therefore, to suggest that an appraisal scheme can be wholly developmental (as some schemes imply), if that means not enquiring into what has already taken place. INSET notwithstanding, most teacher development takes place within the job, in classrooms, in staffrooms, in meetings, in corridors. Therefore it is important to see the ways individual teachers go about the job as potentially vital learning experiences, if only the time and opportunity can be found to distil and then reinforce the learning which inevitably accompanies teacher action. This does not presuppose that teachers will always 'get it right' – indeed many of the most fertile learning experiences stem from initial difficulty or failure – hence the need to make the school a culture in which teachers feel confident enough to experiment with new behaviours and approaches and thus learn and develop from these and grow through experience.

Of course, the way in which the 'review' is conducted is critical: it must not become recriminatory, it should not seek to dwell on problems or failures, but nor can it afford to ignore them. Indeed, the basis of development has at its core the individual maturely accepting responsibility for his or her own previous actions, learning from these, and increasing his or her professional competence as a result.

So whilst the review cannot be left out or glossed over, it will not in itself achieve the purposes of appraisal; it must be used only as a foundation for the planned professional development of the teacher. Thus we have the second component of the appraisal process – planning. Planning which is specific to the teacher and to the situation. Planning which reflects the needs of the individual and of the school, as well as a realistic assessment of ability, time and resources. It is the appraisal interview above all which fuses together these two processes – and so the emphasis placed within the interview will have a major influence on the way the teacher perceives, and so responds to appraisal. In a sense, the problem is locating the interview at an appropriate point on the time continuum which stretches from the beginning of the review period up to the end of the next planning period.

If too much emphasis is placed upon sifting the 'evidence', attempting to produce a definitive account of what it is now too late to alter, then the teacher may very well feel that he or she is simply being 'assessed' – the mutuality and trust necessary for successful appraisal will be damaged, and it is unlikely that future targets identified will be either realistic or motivate the teacher into a real commitment to achieve (Figure 2.10).

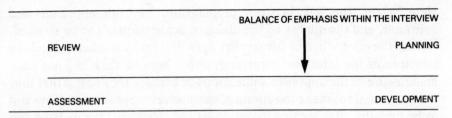

Figure 2.10

Similarly, where appraisers fail to give proper attention to past performance, where they either do not possess the information needed to carry through a systematic review, or (as happens in some cases) have it, but simply fail to use it, it is unlikely that targets set will be realistic (Figure 2.11). It is also possible that the quality of INSET decisions will be poor, as it is difficult to establish training priorities without a systematic review of needs. Often, in these circumstances, the appraisee will feel that the process has been a waste of time – it has not been sufficiently specific to be helpful, it does not lend sharp enough focus to his or her own work and the actual problems and achievements of which the teacher is aware.

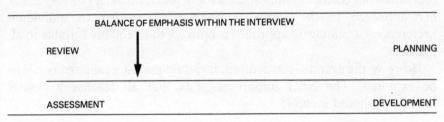

Figure 2.11

Of course, the blending of these two elements can be achieved in a number of ways – it is not necessary to apportion the first half of the interview to 'review', for example (though it may nevertheless sometimes be appropriate to do so), but it is important that the appraiser is constantly aware of the weighting given to each component.

Setting the agenda

This balance is much easier to monitor where there is a clear agenda – an agenda which ideally will have been agreed with the appraisee beforehand, so that he or she has had the opportunity to prepare too.

Here, again, the link between preparation, by both appraisee and appraiser, and the quality of the dialogue achieved needs to be stressed. During the pilot schemes for teacher appraisal many teachers found the structure of the interview surprising, either because they had not been made aware of the appraiser's intentions or because they found that they were expected to 'make the running' themselves; appraisers anxious not to be over-directive seemed happy to let the interview take its pace and structure from the appraisee.

Common approaches to structuring the agenda for the appraisal interview include:

● following the job description of the appraisee
● following a standard structure – eg an interview preparation format
● following a self-appraisal format
● agreeing selected areas for discussion in advance
● following a predetermined interview checklist (eg the NSG advice listed below).

In most cases, it will be possible to choose from a range of approaches. What is important is that the approach adopted is one the appraisee understands and is comfortable with. This means that an appraiser with more than one teacher to appraise may well find it necessary to *vary* his or her approach to the appraisal interview according to individual preference – a 'standard' approach is unlikely to be equally suitable to all teachers.

However the agenda is structured, it should permit a range of issues to be explored. The NSG Report suggests that all teacher appraisal interviews should involve:

- review of the teacher's current job description
- review of the teacher's work, successes and progress in any areas for development identified in the previous appraisal
- discussion of current professional development needs
- discussion of career development as appropriate
- discussion of the appraisee's role in, and contribution to, the policies and management of the school
- identification of targets for future development
- clarification of the points to be recorded in the appraisal statement.

(NSG, 1989)

Again, the order in which these items are tackled, and the relative weighting given to each will necessarily vary according to level and experience of the appraisee and the situation in the school.

Managing the interview

Within the agreed agenda, the interview will need to be managed with skill and sensitivity by the appraiser. There is a growing collection of advice as to how this can best be achieved. Hewton (1988) suggests that the skills required to engage effectively in appraisal interviewing include:

● listening and encouraging the interviewee to talk
● using appropriate questions
● paraphrasing and summarising.

He goes on to argue that appraisers will need training in these skills, as it cannot be assumed that they will have acquired them elsewhere. Diffey (in Fidler and Cooper) underlines the need for the interview to be a *controlled* discussion, and suggests that control is exercised through:

– the relative amount of talking done by each participant
– the tempo of the interview
– the degree of freedom allowed to the appraisee
– the degree to which digression is allowed
– the level of emotional tension or relaxation. (Diffey, 1988)

He suggests further that appraisers should seek 'to control the interview with a loose rein', rather than lean towards over-direction.

Gill, reviewing performance appraisal schemes, concludes that the appraisal interview is most productive when:

– the appraiser adopts a constructive, helpful and supportive approach;
– the appraiser encourages a high level of appraisee participation, particularly in analysing past events and in identifying appropriate targets or goals for the subsequent review period;
– the appraiser favours a problem-solving approach (see Maier, 1976) in which mutuality, trust and joint responsibility are emphasised.

(Gill, 1977)

Clearly then, appraisers will need to give considerable thought to the *style* of the particular appraisal interview. Its *pace*, *structure* and *climate* will all need to be appropriate if the maximum benefits are to be derived from its content. This means that there needs to be planning for the interview itself as well as planning/preparation to ensure that the information needed is available to, and the agenda is understood by, both parties. It also means that appraisers will benefit from opportunities to practise their interview techniques in a context which provides them with feedback on their performance. Training for appraisal should include this element, although it may also be sensible to regard the first run-through of the appraisal process in school as essentially a learning experience, as both appraisers and appraisees will inevitably be nervous. The creation of some forum within school where appraisers can discuss their experiences would help here, and methods of channelling feedback from appraisees into this discussion need to be explored.

Target-setting

A major outcome from the appraisal interview is the setting of appropriate targets for the subsequent review period. Targets need to be identified with particular care, and their status clearly understood. Identifying target areas, for example, does not mean that the rest of the job can be neglected or will not be monitored – targets should be seen rather as agreed priorities, specific tasks or objectives to be achieved within the general routines of the job. As such, it is neither necessary nor desirable to select a large number. It is better to focus on particular priorities deriving from needs or opportunities. Nor is it necessary to identify a range of targets which spread across the full range of responsibilities associated with the job; it is quite normal for different aspects of the job to assume different levels of importance at different times, and target identification should follow this natural pattern of variation. Above all, the targets should be accepted as important by the appraisee. It is vital for motivation and commitment that teachers believe their efforts are being directed towards worthwhile activities.

A commonly used approach to target-setting is the SMART formula; targets should be:

- Specific
- Measurable
- Attainable
- Relevant
- Time-related.

This means ensuring that targets are realistic in terms of the school's ability to provide resources and support, and finite rather than open-ended. It is also important to agree *at the time of target identification* how progress towards that target will be measured, and where possible the information required to monitor progress should subsequently be made available in the same form to both appraiser and appraisee. It should be recognised that though targets will be based on the best knowledge available at the time of the interview, inevitably some will become inappropriate or, at least, need revision because of changes in circumstances during the review period. Some mechanism for reviewing targets and, if necessary, modifying them will therefore be useful between appraisal interviews.

Checklists for appraisers

The following checklists offer some advice to appraisers about various aspects of the interview process which will be useful to those who are new to appraisal.

GENERAL HINTS AND TIPS FOR APPRAISERS

☐ Prepare for the interview, and do what you can to ensure that the appraisee prepares too.

☐ Plan its timing and location so that it takes place in a comfortable and confidential environment and is free from interruptions.

☐ Agree with the appraisee the 'agenda' or areas to be discussed in advance.

☐ Manage the interview rather than dominate it. This means:
  - effective listening
  - appropriate questioning technique
  - avoiding leading and evaluative statements or questions
  - regular summarising of progress and agreements.

☐ Give the appraisee an opportunity to raise any issue or problem which is causing him/her anxiety.

☐ Agree targets or an action plan for the next review period, and check understanding with the appraisee.

☐ Provide a written summary of the main points of the interview as soon as possible, and give the appraisee the opportunity to discuss this before the agreed statement is produced.

☐ Follow up all actions agreed, ensuring that you provide support and resources as well as reviewing progress.

Michael Reddy, in his excellent book *The Manager's Guide to Counselling at Work* (1987), offers a checklist of 'active listening' skills which are likely to be as valuable for appraisers as they are for counsellors.

LISTENING SKILLS

- [ ] paying attention
- [ ] listening to the end of the sentence
- [ ] reflecting
- [ ] echoing
- [ ] expressing feelings
- [ ] checking

- [ ] verifying conclusions
- [ ] clarifying
- [ ] summarising
- [ ] asking for examples
- [ ] encouraging
- [ ] questioning
- [ ] silence.

There are a number of behaviours which are likely to inhibit appraisal dialogue. Appraisers should try to avoid behaviour and responses which lessen the prospects of appraisees talking freely and honestly.

BEHAVIOURS TO AVOID

- [ ] Introducing information at the interview which has not been made available to the appraisee.
- [ ] Jumping from subject to subject or changing the subject without explanation.
- [ ] Showing extreme agreement or disagreement.
- [ ] Focusing on traits or characteristics which the appraisee is unable to alter (eg personality, physical characteristics).
- [ ] Praising or approving of the appraisee's behaviour because it conforms to your own standards.
- [ ] Claiming to know what the appraisee is thinking, or what motivates his/her behaviour.
- [ ] Pressuring/persuading the appraisee to adopt your own views.
- [ ] Over-cosiness.
- [ ] Inappropriate body language.
- [ ] Appearing rushed or pressed for time.

Summary

The interview is at the centre of the appraisal cycle; it needs therefore to be carefully prepared for, sensitively conducted and appropriately followed up if appraisal is to be an effective process. It must not, however, become too 'cosy', the appraisal dialogue should be purposeful and challenging as well as supportive. Appraisers will need therefore to develop the skills necessary to 'manage' the interview, to stimulate meaningful debate and target-setting, and to generate positive responses and attitudes amongst appraisees.

Follow-up Activities

The appraisal statement

The Report of the National Steering Group on the School Teacher Appraisal Pilot Study makes recommendations covering two key areas where post-interview action is required. The first area concerns the production of an agreed *statement*. The previous part of this section has suggested that the appraisal dialogue is likely to include two components – a review of the appraisee's performance in the period since the last appraisal, and a discussion of future plans, developments and targets to be tackled during the next review period. The NSG, advocating a national framework for teacher appraisal, underlines the importance of recording this discussion.

> We recommend that the regulations specify that after each appraisal interview an appraisal statement should be prepared by the appraiser(s), in consultation with the appraisee, recording the main points made in discussion and the conclusion reached, including agreed targets. (NSG, 1989)

The NSG goes on to acknowledge the need to ensure that both appraiser and appraisee are satisfied with the contents of this statement, and where necessary suggests that both parties be able to record their separate views in cases where agreement over particular points is not possible.

Severe disagreement is likely to invalidate the process and the NSG recommended this should be handled via an 'appeals' process which could, for example, offer an alternative appraiser.

The assumption is, however, that in the vast majority of cases the main responsibility for producing this statement will rest with the appraiser, who will need to confirm with the appraisee that the statement is a fair and accurate account of the appraisal dialogue. The format of such a statement, then, must above all seem appropriate to the appraiser and appraisee, and it is likely that any 'standard form' which incorporates more than rudimentary details (eg date, names of appraiser and appraisee) will seem constraining to at least some of those involved. Nevertheless, the pilot schemes threw up considerable evidence that appraisers in particular would welcome some guidance on how to approach the writing up of the interview. This suggests that the training for appraisal will need to engage this issue, and provide potential appraisers with some ways of thinking about it which will help them to develop an organised and systematic approach.

Cummings and Schwab (1973), in an overview of systems for staff appraisal and development, identify three basic approaches which can be modified to help here. They suggest that the major emphasis in post appraisal follow-up can be:

- a developmental action programme (DAP)
- a maintenance action programme (MAP)
- a remedial action programme (RAP).

Though this is probably an artificial separation (as it is likely that in the particular case two or more of these areas could well be appropriate) it may nevertheless provide a useful way of thinking about the drafting of appraisal statements. A remedial action programme, for instance, would require clear feedback from the appraiser indicating why it is felt that the appraisee is experiencing performance difficulty. This would in turn require evidence and address specific incidents or examples. If this approach is extended to embrace more positive aspects of the individual's recent work, again specific examples are likely to be more meaningful to the appraisee than general approval, however expressed. Thus one element of the appraisal statement could be:

(1) An agreed summary of past achievements and difficulties drawing on the evidence available, and where possible, highlighting particular incidents which illustrate the current pattern of strengths and weakness of the appraisee.

A maintenance action programme considers how appraiser and appraisee can best ensure that current strengths and skills are serviced so that satisfactory levels of performance and job satisfaction can be continued. A second element of the appraisal statement then should cover:

(2) Agreed plans and action necessary to help the appraisee maintain his/her current level of competence in relation to the demands of the job.

Obviously, this is most likely to be an important area for concern in times of change, since it is seldom the case that employees are able to maintain performance levels during times of change unless there is some programme of planned support. The relevance of this to the current educational climate and the position of many teachers whose skills and competencies in the classroom relate to a different set of assumptions about the teacher's role will be clear.

A developmental action programme aims at job development and personal growth. It deliberately targets new areas, seeking out new challenges for the appraisee and identifying the necessary action by both appraiser and appraisee to facilitate this development. A third element of the agreed statement therefore would cover:

(3) The establishing of specific targets for personal growth and development together with some indication of how the appraisee's progress in each target area is to be evaluated.

It would, of course, be unwise to attempt too many targets in any given review period.

The agreed statement should then comprise a summary of the appraisal dialogue, recording the main points which have emerged from the review of the appraisee's recent work performance, and linking these into targets and/or action plans as appropriate. Action plans can be targeted on eliminating performance difficulties and generally maintaining individual competence, as well as equipping teachers with new knowledge and/or skills necessary to help them develop their roles within the school.

Appraisers also need to make sure that information contained in the agreed statement, but which is necessary for effective planning at school or LEA level, is made available to the appropriate person. However, this must be done in a way which does not compromise the confidentiality of appraisal records.

> Appraisal statements are personnel documents of a particularly sensitive kind; they should be treated carefully and kept in a secure place in the school. (NSG, 1989)

This means that some information may need, with the appraisee's agreement, to be extracted from the agreed statement and co-ordinated separately within the school. This information would relate to agreed development needs which require support via in-service training, or to targets which had been agreed on the assumption of necessary resources being made available from elsewhere.

The Formal Review meeting

The second major area for post-interview action concerns the need for appraisers and appraisees to continue to be informed by the appraisal dialogue during the review period, and to ensure that both parties take the necessary action to follow through and support agreed priorities and outcomes. Action plans are pursued most effectively when:

● the purpose of the action is clearly identified;
● the nature of the action to be undertaken is accurately described;
● the timing or timescale is identified;
● necessary arrangements to resource/support the action are identified and set in motion;
● the person responsible for making sure the action is carried through is clearly identified;
● methods of evaluating whether the action has in fact met the original purpose are agreed in advance and then used.

The NSG has indicated that it sees this process focused around a 'Formal Review' meeting (this is predicated on the assumption of a two-year appraisal cycle, but if the cycle were to be annual, the processes of review would not change though the need to formalise this meeting may well come into question), which would serve a number of purposes:

– to review the progress of the appraisee and/or the school in meeting professional targets;
– to consider whether targets set at the appraisal interview are still appropriate (the responsibilities of the appraisee may have changed, or factors outside his or her control may have reduced the relevance or feasibility of the targets);
– to consider, where appropriate, the usefulness to date and potential future use of any training undertaken since the appraisal;
– to provide an opportunity for the appraisee to raise any particular issues relating to his or her work;
– to consider the career development needs of the appraisee.

(NSG, 1989)

Clearly, following-up the appraisal dialogue is central to any benefits associated with the process. If both parties do not have a commitment to pursue the actions agreed in the appraisal interview then the scheme will rapidly become an expensive checking exercise of the sort which several research studies would suggest is more likely to reduce motivation and performance levels than to stimulate and to develop. It is therefore highly desirable that there is at least some agreement about and, preferably, some way of monitoring that appropriate follow-up action is taking place. A formal review meeting could do much to support this, though of course it will not compensate for a lack of appropriate action, on a day-to-day basis, by those involved. Thus, while a formal meeting is to be welcomed, it must not become a substitute for follow-up of different kinds.

Though there are many possible follow-up actions which would be appropriate, depending on the situation of the school and the nature of the individual targets, a number of development opportunities are likely to be useful in a range of situations.

Possible follow-up strategies

(i) Specific skills training

The current changes in curriculum content and processes and the introduction of new methods of assessment are tremendously 'de-skilling' for even the most experienced of teachers. It seems likely that, in the short term at least, many teachers will identify targets which relate to the updating of their subject related knowledge and skills. Clearly, then, it will be necessary to identify how this can be achieved effectively and within school budgets. Subject related INSET, both school and LEA led, is one obvious area for action. The appraisal dialogue should identify specific learning requirements and specific learning opportunities – a major aspect of the follow-up will be to ensure that planned activities have taken place and are meeting the need effectively.

(ii) Planned experience

Though course-related training activity has an important strategic role to play in staff development the majority of teacher development takes place within the job. It is very worthwhile therefore to explore how this job-related experience can be used to maximum advantage. Perhaps a change of role (or part of it) would be beneficial. There may be opportunities to use *job rotation* systematically to contribute to a wider pattern of follow-up activities.

Equally, there may be opportunities to increase the autonomy or responsibilities of the appraisee. Can the appraiser increase the level of *delegation*, giving the appraisee the opportunity to extend his or her involvement in decision-making? This is likely to provide the school with a clearer picture of the individual's potential, as well as providing useful experience to the individual.

There may be scope for agreeing with the appraisee a *special project*, an assignment he/she can take on which is outside the normal range of job responsibilities. This may be in an area which is of particular interest to the appraisee (eg subject related investigative work) or meets a current need of the school (eg investigating a cross-curricular theme or issue).

(iii) Focused incidents

It will sometimes be possible to identify a particular task or project which the appraisee will be undertaking during the next review period which can provide a potentially useful learning experience. It is important that the 'incident' is identified in advance, and that the appraisee is reassured that the analysis of how he/she has tackled the situation is to be handled in a constructive and developmental fashion. Given that these safeguards are met, then a systematic analysis of what the appraisee did in the situation, which tries to identify what the alternatives might have been at particular points, what the appraisee was thinking and the reasoning behind any decisions made, can be a most potent development tool. It is also a method of follow-up which requires little in the way of additional resources, though the skills of the appraiser in handling the debriefing will be crucial to its success.

(iv) Coaching

Coaching could be described as on-the-job development, either by the appraiser or by some other experienced teacher. As with focused incidents, it may be possible to identify opportunities for coaching in advance, but whereas in the previous example the emphasis is on allowing the appraisee to make his/her own decision uninfluenced by external advice/support, and only subsequently reviewing these, coaching allows for *active involvement* as the job is done. Thus immediate feedback, advice and encouragement from someone who is experienced in the particular task is at the heart of coaching. It does, therefore, very much like the appraisal interview itself, rely heavily on the interactive and interpersonal skills of the 'coach'.

(v) Management development programmes

Unlike specific skills training, management development seeks to help the individual teacher to acquire those more general skills which are needed to regulate and direct the school in an efficient and effective manner. Most often these have been human/interpersonal skills (eg leadership; team-building) or technical skills (eg timetabling; curriculum analysis). Increasingly, with the advent of local management in schools (LMS), the emphasis is shifting towards the skills necessary to support effective budgetary planning and control. Management development is necessary, both because it is important that schools have available trained staff who can respond to the challenges of school management, and because a significant determinant of the job-satisfaction, of mid- and late-career teachers, will stem from involvement with others teachers in the school, rather than direct contact with pupils. However, evaluating management development activity is difficult – it needs to be viewed as an investment which may take some time to repay. By placing management development on the follow-up agenda from the appraisal process, teachers will be provided with an opportunity to plan for and to discuss the impact of the training in a way which can considerably reduce the amount of uncertainty about its uses and value.

Though by no means exhaustive, the above do offer examples of how the appraisal process can lead to positive action by appraisers and appraisees to ensure that its potential as a developmental tool is harnessed. They also illustrate the kind of discussion which will need to take place at the review meeting – one which is based on the teachers' actions and experiences since the appraisal meeting, rather than one based on a narrow discussion of 'targets'.

Summary

In summary, appropriate follow-up activity is a vital part of the overall appraisal process. This follow-up begins with the (preferably rapid) production of an *'agreed statement'*, which then informs a subsequent programme of actions by appraiser and appraisee in support of agreed priorities and targets. The implementation of this action plan will need to be monitored by the appraiser, and an evaluation of its success, together with a review of targets in light of this, will form the basis of the *review discussion*. In a two year appraisal cycle such review discussions will be necessary within the intervening year to maintain the momentum of the appraisal process. In an annual cycle, the review discussion could very sensibly form the first episode of the next round of appraisal. In this way the original commitment to ensure that appraisal becomes

> ...not a series of perfunctory periodic events, but a continuous and systematic process (Working Group on Appraisal/Training ACAS, 1986)

can best be guaranteed, and maximum benefit can be made available to teacher, to school and, ultimately, to pupils.

SECTION THREE

The Management of Teacher Appraisal

This section looks at the issues involved in managing appraisal at a school level. It consider the tasks involved in establishing and then maintaining an appraisal scheme, and addresses the major issues which have emerged from the individual pilot schemes.

Management of Teacher Appraisal

Teacher appraisal is an important part of the management process: it also needs to be managed. As an aspect of management, appraisal can, we believe, make a significant contribution to the motivation, development and effective use of staff. Given that the staff of a school are its most important and, indeed, most expensive resource, an effective appraisal system is highly desirable to school managers. It is also an aspect of the management role for which managers will need to be trained. Appraisal, when it is simply allowed 'to happen', tends to be haphazard, unsystematic and unproductive. The experience of some schemes reveals how quickly appraisal can become routine, bureaucratic or bland where there is low understanding and commitment. To be effective, appraisal depends both on training in the relevant skills for those who participate and on training in the implementation and running of the process. Skills required include those related to observation and interviewing as well as the development of appropriate staff development skills.

The management of the process as a whole is necessary for a variety of reasons:

- to ensure a scheme is implemented in such a way as to make it 'take hold' in the school;
- to ensure consistency across appraisals and appraisers;
- to ensure the scheme takes place to time and in the manner agreed;
- to ensure targets and outcomes are achieved;
- to evaluate the effectiveness of the scheme.

Tasks involved in establishing and maintaining an appraisal scheme

The table (Figure 3.1) is designed to serve as a checklist of the tasks schools will need to carry out in order to introduce, develop and implement appraisal schemes. In thinking about these tasks the following general points will need to be kept in mind:

55

(1) local/national requirements and guidelines and the consequent degree of flexibility to schools to develop their own approaches;
(2) any previous experience of appraisal and how far a 'new' appraisal scheme will involve changes from previous practice;
(3) the nature of the school's management structure and how it can be linked to the introduction of appraisal;
(4) school values, policies, involvement in other current initiatives and how appraisal might facilitate the work of the school.

Our central point is that while appraisal demands time and energy to work effectively, it should not be seen as an end in itself. Rather it should be seen as a means by which the school can plan more effectively and harmonise the aims of its staff. It provides a unique opportunity to bring individuals together into a team and to help them sort out priorities in a coherent manner. A properly managed appraisal scheme ought to help the implementation of other initiatives.

These points should be kept in mind when referring to the table. Following the table, we develop some of the points made more fully. We then offer some advice on dealing with common problems, which can occur in introducing and implementing appraisal to the particular school.

Clearly, the management of appraisal is likely to vary in complexity according to the size of the school and its situation. The following notes are meant, therefore, to develop the points in the figure, but to serve as a guide only since each school will need to consider its own circumstances.

Prior to implementation

(1) Schools will need to gain *the commitment of teachers* to appraisal. Research evidence suggests that an important determinant of success will be that teachers have the opportunity to adapt appraisal materials to fit the particular school context. There are, of course, certain parameters set out at national and local levels, but we feel that some scope for refinement at school level is necessary to secure commitment to a scheme. Staff can also expect to have influence over the timing and organisation of the scheme. Teachers should, at the very least, be consulted carefully about the purposes, nature and operation of any proposed scheme, but the potential benefits of a wider involvement leading to a real sense of 'ownership' will be obvious to school managers.
(2) It is also important to *provide opportunities for teachers* to discuss concerns and expectations and to clarify the purposes of appraisal.

TASKS INVOLVED IN SETTING UP AN APPRAISAL SCHEME

Prior to Implementation

☐ Securing commitment to appraisal through wide consultation;

☐ Designing (or adapting) a scheme and producing appropriate support materials;

☐ Disseminating information about appraisal and raising awareness;

☐ Integrating appraisal into other initiatives and policies within the school;

☐ Making appropriate arrangements for the management of appraisal including the appointment of appraisers;

☐ Securing a training programme (for all staff) and finding or training trainers;

☐ Ensuring the availability of funding and other necessary resources.

Implementation

☐ Training all staff over a period of time appropriately geared to the introduction;

☐ Providing guidelines to appraisers to ensure a coherent approach;

☐ Providing appropriate support and materials;

☐ Arranging necessary timetabling and support cover;

☐ Dealing with any difficulties or complaints that arise;

☐ Ensuring systems are in place to respond to the outcomes of appraisal;

☐ Arranging for the completion, agreement and storage of appraisal statements.

Monitoring and Evaluation

☐ Setting up appropriate monitoring and evaluation procedures;

☐ Ensuring appeals and complaints procedures are available and understood.

Figure 3.1

(3) A key concern, once a scheme has been designed and is understood by staff, is likely to be over *the matching of appraisers with appraisees*. The options include:

(a) head designates appraisers in line with the management structure of the school;

(b) staff can choose their appraiser, ie 'free' choice;

(c) staff can express a negative preference;

(d) staff can select an appraiser from a panel, selected by the head.

Each of these options has strengths and weaknesses. We would suggest schools discuss the approach they are going to take. Experience suggests above all that the selection of appraisers needs to take into account the following 'ideal' appraiser characteristics:

- someone who has close contact with the appraisee's work;
- someone whom the appraisee regards as credible and experienced;
- someone with a management responsibility for the appraisee.

(4) Schools will need to discuss how appraisal can be *integrated into other activities*. The greater the degree of integration, the more worthwhile appraisal will be. In particular the links between appraisal and School Development Plans will need to be looked at. For example, if a school has already established a set of priorities through development planning, the question is how far can these be promoted and supported through appraisal? Similarly, where teachers are modifying their practice in line with the requirements of National Curriculum, appraisal can provide a vehicle for setting priorities supporting and reviewing progress. Once appraisal is in place, the process itself may well identify areas of individual or school concern, which alter school priorities or require curriculum change. These will need to be addressed in turn. In this respect appraisal can be seen as an important facilitating mechanism.

(5) Schools will need to ensure *the appropriate management of appraisal*. In the School Teacher Appraisal Pilot Study, the way that appraisal was managed tended to reflect the size of the school. Two key aspects emerged. First the identification of a *co-ordination role*, to be carried out either by the head and/or by another teacher, according to the size of the school. Essentially this role involved:

- liaison between the school and the LEA/external trainers/evaluators etc;
- taking a lead in the design, planning and implementation of the scheme;

- **organising a timetable** for the process and arranging the necessary supply cover;
- monitoring the process and ensuring consistency;
- arranging for the production, completion and storage of appropriate documentation;
- ensuring that outcomes and targets are followed-up;
- dealing with complaints and ensuring that the process is carried out as agreed.

In deciding on how to allocate these tasks, the school will need to consider both school size and the existing approach to management. It may be appropriate to split these tasks between individuals. For example, a deputy with time-tabling/cover responsibilities could take on those aspects of appraisal, while a deputy with INSET responsibilities could take on responsibility for ensuring that the outcomes of appraisal were supported. The Head may also decide to introduce a 'grandparent' interview option, ie the appraiser's appraiser can hold a second interview with an appraisee should a complaint be made or as a monitoring device. This can serve as an 'in-house' mechanism for dealing with any complaint which cannot be settled by further discussion between the appraisee and the appraiser.

In addition to the co-ordination role, the pilot study saw the emergence of a second aspect of management for appraisal – *the school working group*. Basically, when this appeared, it took the form of a representative group of staff, who advised the school on the design and implementation of the scheme. Beyond the pilot study, it may be that schools already have appropriate committees in place for this task. We would see it as important, however, that the management of appraisal allows for the development of the scheme in the light of the real experiences of the teachers involved.

Implementation

(1) Schools will need to ensure that teachers receive appropriate training and that 'off-site' training and appropriate 'in-school' work are co-ordinated.

(2) The Head/Co-ordinator must arrange an appraisal timetable, organise supply cover, arrange for monitoring of the scheme and make arrangements for handling of documentation.

(3) Appraisers and appraisees need to be provided with support, materials and guidance as required.

Monitoring and evaluation

(1) Schools will need to monitor their scheme.
- Are the components being carried out when agreed and in the manner agreed?
(If not, how is this dealt with?)
(2) Schools will need to evaluate their scheme.
- Is the scheme achieving the purposes set out for it?
(How can this be judged? If not, how is this dealt with?)

This area is considered in more detail in Section Five.

Issues which the management of appraisal may need to address

Reservations about the appraiser

An appraisee's attitude towards his or her appraiser tends to determine attitudes to the process as a whole. Whatever approach to the allocation of appraisers is taken, Heads need to be sensitive to possible mismatches. The following options may be worth considering in case of difficulties.

● Can the appraiser and appraisee be persuaded to 'give it a go'? This might be worth doing if their problems stem from lack of communication. In cases of that type, an uninterrupted appraisal interview *might* be productive.
● Can the appraisal role be divided? For example, could observation be carried out by another colleague, with the appraiser carrying out the interview?
● Is the reassurance of a 'grandparent' interview, if required, likely to overcome reservations in some cases?
● Is there some way of convincing appraiser/appraisee pairs that mutual trust and understanding are often increased as a result of appraisal?
● Is there a possible alternative appraiser and would the use of the alternative overcome the problem?

Time

Appraisal takes time and energy. The following points may help, if not to change that fact, at least to keep the demands within reasonable bounds.

● How far are the components of appraisal being carried out already and how far do they represent new demands? Can some established activities be replaced by the various parts of the appraisal process?

- Appraisal can help to bring staff together as a team, creating a shared view of priorities and a sense of purpose. It can also improve communication. How much time will this save in the long run by cutting out misunderstandings and people working at cross-purposes?
- Is it possible to secure the services of regular supply teachers to release people for appraisal and to minimise disruption to classes?
- Can appraisal be timetabled on a 'rolling' basis, so as to ensure that no appraiser is involved in too much appraisal activity at any one time?
- Can the various appraisal tasks be split (eg by delegating some classroom/task observation, or by having appraisees prepare their own statements) so as to spread the workload?

Confidentiality

It is likely that concerns about the use of appraisal documents and access to them will surface at an early stage. We recommend that the issues arising are discussed with staff and that everyone is clear about the relevant ground rules, before starting the process. The following points may be worth considering:

- A division can be made between working documents (eg observation notes) created during the process and the final agreed interview statement. The former documents might be seen as existing only until the appraisal process has been completed, whereas the agreed statement would remain in existence for a longer period.
- The agreed statement summary could be produced in parts. The first part could be a summary of the interview discussion as a whole, and the second part could list targets and plans that have emerged. Different rules for access could be written for each part.

Summary

The management of appraisal is, like appraisal, a means to an end. It is designed to ensure that the process serves agreed purposes and benefits the school. The more the management of appraisal and the process itself can be integrated into other school activities the better appraisal will serve its purposes.

SECTION FOUR

Support Documentation

This section outlines the major forms of documentation necessary to support the introduction and maintenance of a teacher appraisal scheme. It lists a number of useful sources for appraisal related documents and offers advice on points to bear in mind when devising the paper-work which accompanies the appraisal process.

SECTION FOUR

INQUIRY AND EXPLANATION

Support Documentation

Our purpose in this section is to review the type of documentation that can help the appraisal process to run smoothly. It is, of course, vital that appraisal is not allowed to degenerate into a routine and largely bureaucratic exercise. Documentation must *serve* the process, not lead it. We would stress therefore the importance of adapting approaches to suit the particular school and of monitoring the usefulness of all documentation used to ensure that the danger of appraisal becoming a burdensome paper exercise can be minimised.

What documentation is needed in appraisal?

Appraisal documentation can be divided into the following categories:

(1) *Explanatory materials*: handbooks, manuals etc, designed to explain the philosophy, purposes, ground rules and nature of the appraisal scheme and to make people aware of basic legal, ethical and practical requirements.
(2) *Support materials*: pro-formas designed to support particular stages or aspects of the process, eg self-appraisal forms, observation forms/schedules, interview preparation forms.
(3) *The appraisal statement form*: a record of the main points discussed during the appraisal interview and a note of action plans or targets agreed for the future.
(4) *System maintenance materials*: these can take the form of reminders of when particular stages of the process are to take place. They also include pro-formas designed to log and to monitor the process.

Schools will need to consider the requirements in each category when setting up appraisal schemes. The task will be made easier if attention is paid to achieving consistency across the categories and, if possible, using the same basic form for a variety of purposes.

Explanatory materials

The production of explanatory materials can benefit from the significant work already done in this area. In the School Teacher Appraisal Pilot Study, the pilot LEAs prepared handbooks to explain and support their schemes. These provide one source of materials which may be helpful in preparing a handbook for school use. Such handbooks may also draw on the following published sources (which are listed in full in the References section of this book): ACAS (1986) *Report of the Appraisal/Training Working Group*; HMI (1989) *Developments in the Appraisal of Teachers*; Bradley *et al.* (1989) *Report on the Evaluation of the School Teacher Appraisal Study*; NSG (1989) *School Teacher Appraisal: A National Framework*. It will of course, be necessary to take account of any guidance on appraisal, from the DES (expected in the Summer term of 1990), any regulations, which may subsequently be published and emerging LEA advice.

Handbooks will need to clarify a number of aspects of the appraisal process. It is essential for those embarking on appraisal to have a clear and shared understanding of the processes and requirements if difficulties are to be avoided. Aspects to be addressed include:

- the purposes of the process;
- the components of the process;
- the use of criteria;
- ground rules concerning: the selection of appraisers, arrangements for handling disagreements or complaints, procedures for gathering data and the use of appraisal documentation;
- practical issues relating to the timespan, frequency and organisation of the scheme.

Support materials

Elsewhere in this book (see Appendix 1) are a variety of examples of forms and pro-formas which can be used to support particular aspects of the appraisal process. We have included pro-formas for use in self-appraisal; classroom observation; and other aspects of the process.

We see such forms as working documents which serve appraisers and appraisees and which have no further use once the appraisal process is complete. We have, also, stressed the importance of schools developing and adapting forms for use in these areas in order to devise something that is seen locally as relevant and appropriate. Involvement in this design process may also enable a sense of ownership and commitment to be developed.

The following questions will need to be addressed during this process of design:

- Is the form easy to use?
- How far does the form prompt the user to assemble facts or make judgements?
- Does the form relate to specific points or seek to cover a wide range of aspects of the job?

Our view is that forms should be simple, 'home-grown', specific and dealing in facts, unless there are identified reasons for varying from this.

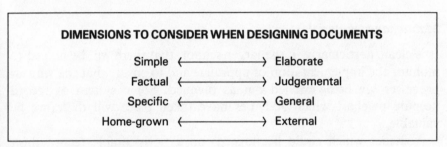

The appraisal statement form

Each appraisal interview should result in an agreed statement. We believe that this can most usefully be divided into two major sections – the first section summarising key points raised in the discussion, the second recording targets and action plans for the future. In practice both sections are designed to provide a record of what was agreed so that those involved in the process have a clear point of reference when they come subsequently to discuss how far targets have been achieved, or when they begin the next appraisal cycle. The statement needs to be viewed as a two-way document; both appraiser and appraisee need to make a commitment to act upon it. To emphasise these points, the two major sections should be followed by places for both appraiser and appraisee to sign the statement and for any additional comments the appraisee wishes to make. There are, therefore, a number of stages to be worked through:

(1) Either appraiser or appraisee can draft the appraisal statement, but both need to check the statement and agree it. A time will be needed for this.

(2) Most often disagreements stem from misunderstanding and can be accommodated by an agreed modification to the draft. (This was

the experience of the School Teacher Appraisal Pilot Study.) Should this not be possible, the appraisee may wish to add an additional note, setting out the nature of his/her disagreement. Beyond that, appeals or complaints procedures are likely to be involved.

(3) The section on targets should state clearly what the targets are, when they are to be achieved, what the support implications are and who has responsibility for following up on them.

(4) Where the appraiser is not the headteacher, or where targets proposed are dependent on action by a third person, steps will need to be taken to gain this person's commitment and support. It should be made clear at the interview *whose responsibility* it is to gain this approval.

Maintenance materials

It is clear, particularly in the larger school, that there will be a need to monitor the implementation of appraisal and to ensure that the various processes are being carried out as planned. Some system of record keeping to chart which activities have taken place will therefore be valuable.

Activities which could be 'logged' on a fairly simple record sheet include classroom observation sessions, appraiser/appraisee meetings, including the appraisal interview, and the completion of Appraisal Statements. Examples of how this could be done are included in Appendix 1.

Conclusion

As we indicated at the beginning of this section, documentation for appraisal should serve and not dictate the process. It should also be consistent with the school's normal approach to documentation. The aim should be to ensure the smooth running of the appraisal process and to tie it into the normal working of the school, not to create a new industry.

SECTION FIVE

Monitoring and Evaluation

This section suggests how a number of aspects of the appraisal process can be monitored and evaluated within the school. The emphasis is on approaches which are economical to administer and provide a basis for individual and whole school reflection without requiring the collation of masses of forms.

Monitoring and Evaluation

Monitoring

It will be necessary to monitor the implementation of teacher appraisal within the school. Obviously, no judgements can be made about the impact of appraisal until it is established that the scheme is being carried out as planned. The school will therefore need, first of all, to devise some way of monitoring that the agreed activities are taking place; it will then be possible to evaluate its contribution to the school. One way of doing this, which might bring with it the added bonus of reminding staff what they need to do, is to produce a simple form on which the various stages and activities within the appraisal process can be logged as they take place. Appendix 1 includes one example of a form which can be used for this purpose (Document 10 Activity Monitoring Form) which can be filled in by the appraiser as the various stages of the process are completed.

Evaluation

In order to ensure that teacher appraisal is beneficial for the school it will be necessary to evaluate a number of aspects. These will include the processes which make up appraisal, the way the scheme is managed within the school, and the extent to which the intended outcomes are being achieved.

Processes

Though there are a number of processes within appraisal which are important, the evidence collected during the teacher appraisal pilot schemes suggested that the most important requirement for an effective appraisal dialogue was adequate preparation by both parties. Clearly, the amount and quality of preparation can be evaluated via several methods.

However, within the school a balance must be struck between the cost of evaluating (in time and effort) and the potential benefits of evaluation data. Sensible use of self-evaluation is therefore an attractive and low-cost strategy, which seems particularly appropriate to preparation activities.

The checklist in Figure 5.1 simply suggests how a self evaluation pro-forma might be used to prompt reflection and development, and it is not intended to be prescriptive. Figures 5.2 and 5.3 show how a similar approach could be used to help appraisees evaluate their contributions to and benefits from appraisal.

Outcomes

In the longer term, it will be important to check that teacher appraisal is producing the expected outcomes. Obviously, the specific outcomes sought will vary from school to school, though there may well be common elements. In evaluating the extent to which outcomes are being realised, the school will need to go back to its own statement of purposes. Using the purposes suggested in the first section as an example, a format for evaluating outcomes could be developed using the questions listed in Figures 5.4 and 5.5.

Summary

The examples above are not intended to be prescriptive though it is hoped that they will help schools to distinguish between monitoring and evaluation activities, and provide start points for the school's own activity in these areas. The important issue to keep in sight is that it is not 'doing teacher appraisal' which matters, but finding within teacher appraisal a vehicle for meeting and contributing to the development of school and teacher goals. This is the issue on which evaluation should focus.

APPRAISER SELF EVALUATION CHECKLIST

Was I properly informed?

☐ Did I gain a true picture of how the appraisee does his/her job, including any problems or difficulties faced?

☐ Did I pay enough attention to the non-teaching aspects of the job?

☐ Did I make sure that the appraisee was aware of the information I was seeking and encourage him/her to contribute?

Did I handle classroom observation satisfactorily?

☐ Was there an agreed focus?

☐ Were the method(s) of observation and recording discussed and agreed?

☐ Was an appropriate occasion(s) identified, giving the appraisee plenty of notice?

☐ Was there a proper debriefing of the appraisee within a day or two of the observation?

How well did I prepare for the interview?

☐ Did I have all the relevant information?

☐ Had I thought through how to use the information?

☐ Was the appraisee made aware of the agenda in advance?

Did I plan the interview properly?

☐ Was enough time made available?

☐ Was the appraisee freed from work pressures?

☐ Was the environment suitable and free from interruptions/distractions?

Did I handle the interview satisfactorily?

☐ Did the appraisee seem comfortable/relaxed?

☐ Was the balance of talking/listening satisfactory?

☐ Was the quality of listening high?

☐ Were we able to tackle difficult areas?

☐ Did the appraisee seem happy with the way the discussion was conducted?

Did I close the interview satisfactorily?

☐ Did I summarise the discussions for the benefit of the appraisee?

☐ Did I ensure that there was agreement over the main points of discussion?

☐ Did I secure agreement over appropriate targets?

☐ Did I leave the appraisee feeling optimistic and committed to achieving agreed targets?

Am I prepared for the necessary follow-up activities?

☐ What is required of me?

☐ What should I be organising through others?

☐ What contact/support should I make available to the appraisee before the next review?

Figure 5.1

APPRAISEE EVALUATION SHEET (1)

How useful was:
The initial meeting?

Conducting self-appraisal?

Classroom/Task observation?

Preparing for the appraisal interview?

The interview itself?

Any follow-up action since?

Figure 5.2

APPRAISEE EVALUATION SHEET (2)	
The Interview	
What outcomes did I hope to gain from the interview?	Were these achieved?
What was I most pleased about?	Factors that contributed
What was I least happy with?	Factors that contributed
What would I do differently next time?	How will this improve the process?
What would I like my appraiser to do differently next time?	How will this improve the process?

Figure 5.3 (Based on a format suggested by Carroll and Nuttall, 1989)

IMPACT ON THE SCHOOL

Do you feel that appraisal has:

Helped us to refine our objectives and priorities?

Improved planning processes?

Improved communication within the school?

Improved relationships between staff members?

Led to a better use of resources?

Supported major developments within the school?

Figure 5.4 (To be completed by all teaching staff)

IMPACT ON THE TEACHERS

Do you feel that appraisal has:

Improved your confidence/competence in your present role?

Improved your working relationships with colleagues?

Given you appropriate feedback on your strengths and weaknesses?

Supported you in developing your professional practice?

Given you an opportunity to influence school, departmental and personal goals?

Encouraged you to develop your skills and prepare for promotion?

Increased your level of satisfaction with your work and the way you do it?

Improved your understanding of the school and your own role within it?

Figure 5.5 (To be completed by all teaching staff)

References

ACAS (1986) *Report of the Appraisal/Training Working Group*. London: ACAS.

Bradley, H. W. *et al.* (1989) *Report on the Evaluation of the School Teacher Appraisal Pilot Study*. Cambridge: Cambridge Institute of Education.

Bollington, R., Hopkins, D. and West, M. (1990) *An Introduction to Teacher Appraisal*. London: Cassell.

Carroll, S. and Nuttall, S. (1989) *Managing Staff Development – Policy into Practice*. Lancaster: Framework Press.

Cummings, L. L. and Schwab, D. P. (1973) *Performance in Organisations – determinants and appraisal*. Illinois: Scott, Foresman and Co.

Fidler, B. and Cooper, R. (eds) (1988) *Staff Appraisal in Schools and Colleges*. Harlow: Longman.

Gill, D. (1977) *Appraising Performance*. London: IPM.

HMI (1989) *Developments in the Appraisal of Teachers*. London: DES.

Hewton, E. (1988) *The Appraisal Interview*. Milton Keynes: Open University Press.

Heywood, J. (1989) Taking a Long Look. In *Education Guardian 24 October 1989*. London: Guardian.

MacGregor, J. (1989) *Speech to the Secondary Heads Association*. London: DES Press Office.

National Steering Group (NSG) on School Teacher Appraisal (1989) *School Teacher Appraisal – A National Framework*. London: HMSO.

Philp, T. (1983) *Making Performance Appraisal Work*. London: McGraw Hill.

Rackham, J., Honey, P. and Colbert, M. (eds) (1973) *Developing Interactive Skills*. Northampton, Wellens.

Reddy, M. (1987) *The Managers Guide to Counselling at Work*. London: Methuen.

Suffolk Education Department (1988) *Teacher Appraisal – The Way Forward*. Ipswich: Suffolk County Council.

APPENDIX ONE

Sample Documents

This section is made up of a number of sample documents which could be used to support the various aspects of the appraisal process. These are put forward as starting points for the development of appropriate approaches and formats, and readers should feel free to adapt and modify them as they see fit in order to match the needs of their own school.

Readers may copy the documents in this Appendix for use within their own schools though they remain the copyright property of the authors and should not be copied or distributed for other purposes without prior permission from the publishers. The documents include:

1. Initial Meeting – Suggested Agenda
2. Self-appraisal Prompt Sheet
3. Self-appraisal Question Sheet
4. Classroom Observation Schedule
5. Teacher-Pupil Interaction Tally Sheet
6. Interview Preparation Form
7. Agreed Statement
8. Cover Request Form
9. Monitoring Interview Request Form
10. Activity Monitoring Form

1. Initial meeting – suggested Agenda

AGENDA

(1) Nature and purposes of appraisal.

(2) Focus of appraisal.

(3) Information needed to prepare for interview

  – data gathering approaches
  – arrangements for these.

(4) Dates and timetabling of the rest of the process.

(5) AOB.

2. Self-appraisal prompt sheet

SELF-APPRAISAL PROMPT SHEET

Please reflect on each of the following aspects of teaching which apply to you. Consider how happy and confident you feel with each aspect. Also consider what steps could be taken by you and by others to bring about improvements, when you feel these are needed.

(1) CLASSROOM WORK

(a) **General overview**

General atmosphere in lessons
Quality of relationships
Interest aroused
Attention by you to pupils of varying needs
General class control
Confidence in subject matter

(b) **Preparation**

Curriculum planning/development
Preparation of schemes of work
Preparation for individual lessons
Linking lessons to each other

(c) **Classroom management**

Use of a variety of teaching strategies
Clarity of expectations/instructions
Pace and timing
Availability of necessary resources
Suitability of work to pupils
Degree of pupil responsibility
Organisation of room and resources

(d) **Follow-up**

Maintenance of pupil records
Marking/giving feedback to pupils
Setting homework/coursework
Evaluating courses/lessons

---

(2) MANAGEMENT WORK

Keeping up to date with new developments/initiatives
Planning and determining policy
Setting objectives, goals and targets
Organising and utilising resources
Monitoring objectives/evaluation
Motivating others/staff development
Providing feedback to staff
Use of various means of communication
Use of time
Liaison with relevant colleagues

Self-appraisal prompt sheet cont/d

(3) PASTORAL WORK
Relationships
Development of a pastoral programme/use of tutorial time
Liaison with relevant colleagues
Awareness of individual pupils
Maintenance of appropriate records

(4) OTHER ASPECTS OF YOUR WORK
Please add below any other prompts you feel would be helpful.

84

3. Self-appraisal question sheet

SELF-APPRAISAL QUESTIONS

I feel my work would improve most if...

I am happiest with my work in..

The area of my work I am least happy with is..

The main constraints affecting my work are...

The pupils I achieve the most with are..

The pupils I achieve the least with are..

The colleagues I work with are...

The actions I would most like to see my headteacher take are............................

My work links to the SDP in terms of..

My immediate priorities in my job are...

My career aims are...

I would like to develop further professionally by...

What I hope for most from appraisal is..

4. Classroom observation schedule

CLASSROOM OBSERVATION SCHEDULE

Please record as factually and objectively as possible key events in each of the
following aspects of classroom work, that have previously been agreed as points
of focus.

Teaching strategies used

Use and organisation of resources

Pupil response and understanding

Relationships

Involvement of pupils

Learning experiences available

Marking and assessment

Teacher's instructions/expectations/language

Subject matter

---

5. Teacher–pupil interaction tally sheet

CLASSROOM OBSERVATION

Please place a tick by each of the behaviours listed below, *each* time it occurs. The aim is to build up an accurate pattern of classroom events.

Teacher	Total
Use of praise	
Non-verbal communication	
Use of reprimand	
Giving instructions	
Questions to named individuals	
Questions to whole class	
Answering questions	
Pupils	
Individuals asking questions of teacher	
Individuals making statements/giving information	
Individuals expressing opinions	
Individuals exhibiting negative behaviour	

6. Interview preparation form

INTERVIEW PREPARATION FORM/AGENDA

1. Is your job description accurate? Are any modifications necessary? How does your work relate to the SDP?

2. What aspects of your work have you been particularly pleased with since your last appraisal interview? What success have you had in working on the targets set during your last appraisal?

3. What aspects of your work have not gone as well as you hoped? What difficulties have you experienced in work on the targets set during your last appraisal?

4. What constraints have affected your work? Can you suggest any ways in which these might be overcome?

5. Please identify your main priorities and targets for the next year and any INSET or other support you need in connection with as many of the following areas as are appropriate.
   (a) your present job

   (b) your general professional development

   (c) your career aims

6. Are there any points you wish to discuss?

---

7. Agreed statement

AGREED STATEMENT

Section 1
(a) Job description/links of job with SDP

(b) Areas of success

(c) Areas for further development

(d) Constraints

(e) Other points covered:

Agreed Statement cont/d

Section 2   AGREED TARGETS/PLANS FOR FUTURE ACTION

Name of appraisee...............   Name of appraiser...............   Date...............

Target area	Target/action plan	Resource implications	Date for completion	Support needed from:	Success criteria	Other comments
Present job						
General professional						
Career related						

Agreed Statement cont/d

Section 3

We have both read Sections 1 and 2 of this statement and accept it as a true and fair record of our discussions.

Signed... Apraisee

Signed... Appraiser

Date ....

Section 4

The appraisee may add below any additional comments he or she wishes to make.

Signed... Date ....

We have indicated previously that someone within each school will need to co-ordinate the appraisal process. The responsibility is likely to include timetabling the process and arranging supply cover, monitoring the process and ensuring it takes place in a consistent and agreed manner. The following documentation may prove useful in facilitating these tasks.

8. Cover request form

TEACHER APPRAISAL SCHEME COVER REQUEST

(Please hand to the Appraisal Co-ordinator at least two weeks before the date cover is needed)

Could you please arrange supply cover from _____ to _____

on _____, to allow us to carry out _____.

This will be needed by _____

Approved/Not Approved

Signed _____ (Appraisal Co-ordinator)

---

9. Monitoring interview request form

TEACHER APPRAISAL SCHEME

_____ would like to see you on _____ at

_____ to discuss your participation in the school's appraisal scheme.

---

10. Activity monitoring form

RECORD OF APPRAISAL ACTIVITIES

Name of Appraisee _____

Name of Appraiser _____

Opening date of appraisal cycle _____

Closing date of appraisal cycle _____

		Time/Date to be carried out	Tick to show carried out	Comments
Initial meeting				
Self Appraisal				
Classroom observation	1			
	2			
	3			
Task observation	1			
	2			
	3			
Collecting colleagues' views				
Interview				
Production of statement				
Follow-up meetings				
Review meetings	1			
	2			
	3			
Other components (please specify)				

APPENDIX TWO

Code of Practice

This section reproduces the Guidance and Code of Practice on the Collection of Information for Teacher and Head Teacher Appraisal from the National Steering Group report *School Teacher Appraisal – A National Framework* (1989). It is reproduced with the permission of HMSO.

Guidance and Code of Practice on the Collection of Information for Teacher and Head Teacher Appraisal

1. This guidance and Code of Practice covers the collection of information for teacher and head teacher appraisal other than through classroom observation.

General principles

2. Information collection for the purpose of the appraisal of a teacher or head teacher should be designed to assist discussion in an appraisal interview having the purposes set out in paragraphs 40–43 and 57.
3. Where it has been agreed that the appraisal should concentrate on specific aspects of the appraisee's job, information collection should likewise concentrate on those aspects.
4. Appraisers should act with sensitivity to all concerned and should not exhibit any bias in collecting information.
5. Those giving information should not be put under any pressure save that of relevance and accuracy.
6. General comments should be supported by specific examples.
7. Interviews for the purpose of information collecion should be held on a one to one basis.
8. Any information received anonymously should not be used.
9. Information which does not relate to the professional performance of a teacher or head teacher should not be sought or accepted.
10. Appraisees should not adopt an obstructive attitude to reasonable proposals for the collection of appropriate information.
11. Neither appraisers nor appraisees should act in any way that is likely to threaten the trust and confidence on both sides upon which successful appraisal depends.

Background information

Teacher appraisal

12. The teacher's appraiser must be familiar with relevant national and LEA policies and requirements.
13. The appraiser will also need to acquire a range of background information appropriate to the appraisee's wider professional responsibilities, e.g. the school's statements of aims and objectives, pastoral arrangements, equal opportunities policies, or departmental policies.
14. The appraiser should obtain copies of the teacher's job description and of the previous appraisal statement.

Head teacher appraisal

15. The head teacher's appraisers must be familiar with current national and LEA policies and requirements with regard to curriculum, special needs, equal opportunities, staffing and cover, disciplinary and grievance procedures and other such matters relating to school management.
16. They will also need a wide range of background information about the school and its context including:

    curricular policies
    general organisation and deployment of staff
    composition and organisation of the governing body
    links with home, outside bodies and other schools
    the pattern of meetings with staff and with parents.
    school activities and routines including assessment and
        recording systems, examination results, calendar of events
    staff appraisal and development arrangements and
        arrangements for induction and probation
    financial and management systems

    This information will need to be assembled by appraisee heads, who may provide any supplementary information they wish.
17. The appraisers should obtain copies of the head teacher's job description and of the previous appraisal statement.

Other guidance to the appraiser

18. The appraiser should agree with the appraisee at the initial meeting what information it would be appropriate to collect for the purpose of the appraisal, from what sources and by what methods.
19. When interviewing people providing information as part of an appraisal, the appraiser should explain the purpose of the interview and the way in which information will be treated.
20. Those giving information should be encouraged to make fair and considered comments which they are prepared to acknowledge and to substantiate if required.
21. Any written submissions should remain confidential to the author, the appraiser and the appraisee.
22. Those offering significantly critical comments should be asked to discuss them directly with the appraisee before they are used as appraisal information. (The substance of grievance or disciplinary proceedings should never be used in the appraisal process.)
23. Except where personal opinion is specifically sought (for example where an appraiser is attempting to gauge staff reactions to a particular innovation), care should be taken to ensure that information is sought and presented in an objective way.

Reproduced with the permission of the Controller of HMS.O.

Key Points Index

ACAS, 3, 6, 21, 22, 24, 34, 52, 56
Appraisal Statement, 16, 45, 47, 51,
   61, 65, 67, 88–90

Classroom Observation, 15, 16, 20,
   24–26, 30, 83
Code of Practice, 33, 95–97
Complaints, 45, 58, 68
Confidentiality, 11, 61
Coordinator, 10, 58

Documentation, 59, 61, 65–68

Evaluation, 5, 22, 59, 71–75

Feedback, 5, 23, 25, 28, 29, 33
Focus, 17, 18, 20, 25, 36, 81

Information gathering, 19, 20, 33, 36
INSET, 8, 38, 39, 49, 58
Interview, 15, 16, 29, 34, 37–44, 74

Management, 8, 41, 44, 53–61

Objectives, 11

National Steering Group, 7, 16, 33,
   37, 40, 45, 47, 48, 66

Purposes, 1–11, 20, 30, 57
Preparation, 15–17, 34, 40, 87

Records, 68, 91
Resources, 11, 38, 47
Review discussion, 36, 38, 48, 51

School Teacher Appraisal Pilot
   Study, 3, 10, 16, 20, 28, 30, 58, 66
Self-appraisal, 20–23, 82, 84

Target-setting, 15, 16, 29, 40, 42, 44,
   47, 48, 68
Task observation, 20, 29, 30
Time, 19, 21, 38, 48, 56–60
Training, 41, 46–48, 59

Notes